A Griffith History

A Griffith History

How the House at Pound Ridge was Built

JENNIFER GRIFFITH BLACK

Genealogy House
Amherst, Massachusetts

First published 2021 by Genealogy House, a division of White River Press
PO Box 3561, Amherst, MA 01004 • www. genealogyhouse.net

ISBN: 978-1-887043-93-9

Book and cover design by Douglas Lufkin of Lufkin Graphic Designs
Norwich, Vermont 05055 • www.lufkingraphics.com

Library of Congress Cataloging-in-Publication Data

Names: Black, Jennifer Griffith, 1963- author.
Title: A Griffith history / Jennifer Griffith Black.
Description: Amherst, Massachusetts : Genealogy House, [2021] | Includes
    index. | Summary: "A Griffith History is a genealogy of the author's
    family, focusing on the family of Isaac Griffith and Eliza Curtis in the
    beginning of the 18th century in My Lady's Manor, Baltimore County,
    Maryland, and their descendants, including the families of those
    marrying into the Griffith family"-- Provided by publisher.
Identifiers: LCCN 2021009798 | ISBN 9781887043939 (hardcover)
Subjects: LCSH: Griffith family. | Baltimore County (Md.)--Genealogy. |
    Griffith, Isaac, 1813-1866--Family.
Classification: LCC CS71.G85 2021 | DDC 929.20973--dc23
LC record available at https://lccn.loc.gov/2021009798

Dedication

While the history of the Griffith family began a long time ago, it continues to be written with each generation. This book is dedicated with love to Sage, Amalie, Henry, Bray, Jack, Susie, Tommy, McKenzie, Carson and Kathryn, and all the other Griffiths to come, because they will be the ones to carry the Griffith History forward, with gratitude to Penny and Alan, for sharing Piney Point with all of us to add so many memories to our family story, and in loving memory of Gammy, Grandpa and the house at Pound Ridge.

A locket belonging to Nellie Frances Phillips, which was sent to the author during the research for this book

Contents

Griffith Family
(Direct Ancestors)

Ancestors of Charles Ernest Griffith Sr. and Amalie Louise Guenther

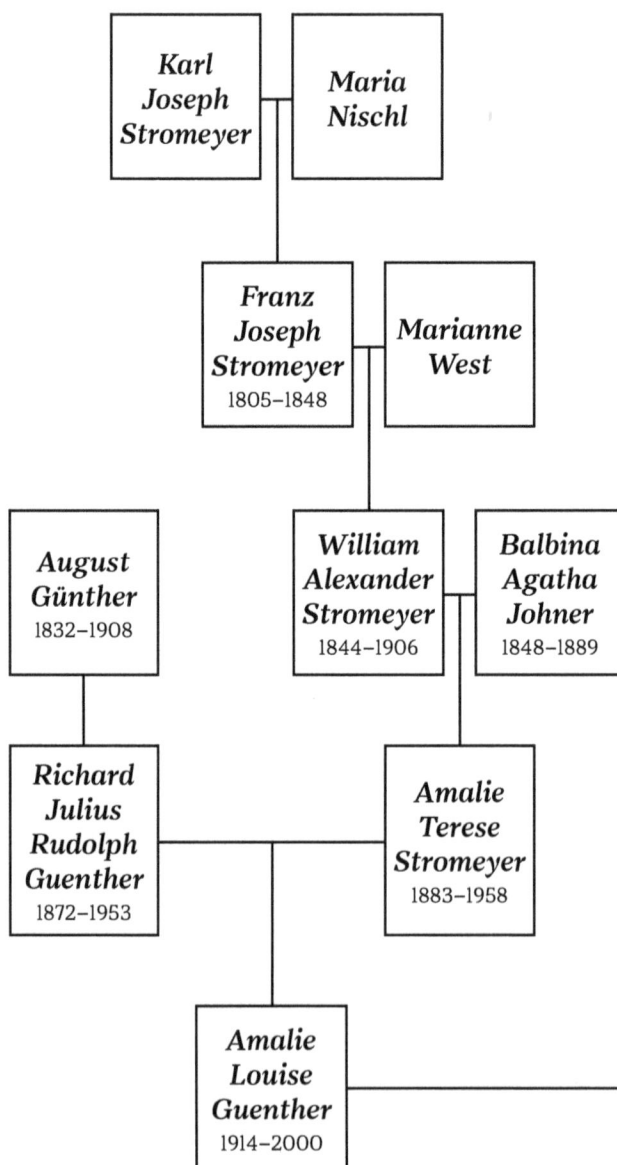

```
┌─────────────────┐  ┌─────────────┐
│      Karl       │  │    Maria    │
│     Joseph      │  │   Nischl    │
│    Stromeyer    │  │             │
└─────────────────┘  └─────────────┘

        ┌──────────────┐  ┌──────────────┐
        │    Franz     │  │   Marianne   │
        │    Joseph    │  │     West     │
        │   Stromeyer  │  │              │
        │   1805–1848  │  │              │
        └──────────────┘  └──────────────┘

┌─────────────┐  ┌──────────────┐  ┌─────────────┐
│   August    │  │   William    │  │   Balbina   │
│   Günther   │  │  Alexander   │  │   Agatha    │
│  1832–1908  │  │  Stromeyer   │  │   Johner    │
│             │  │  1844–1906   │  │  1848–1889  │
└─────────────┘  └──────────────┘  └─────────────┘

┌─────────────┐        ┌─────────────┐
│   Richard   │        │   Amalie    │
│   Julius    │        │   Terese    │
│   Rudolph   │        │  Stromeyer  │
│   Guenther  │        │  1883–1958  │
│  1872–1953  │        │             │
└─────────────┘        └─────────────┘

        ┌─────────────┐
        │   Amalie    │
        │   Louise    │
        │  Guenther   │
        │  1914–2000  │
        └─────────────┘
```

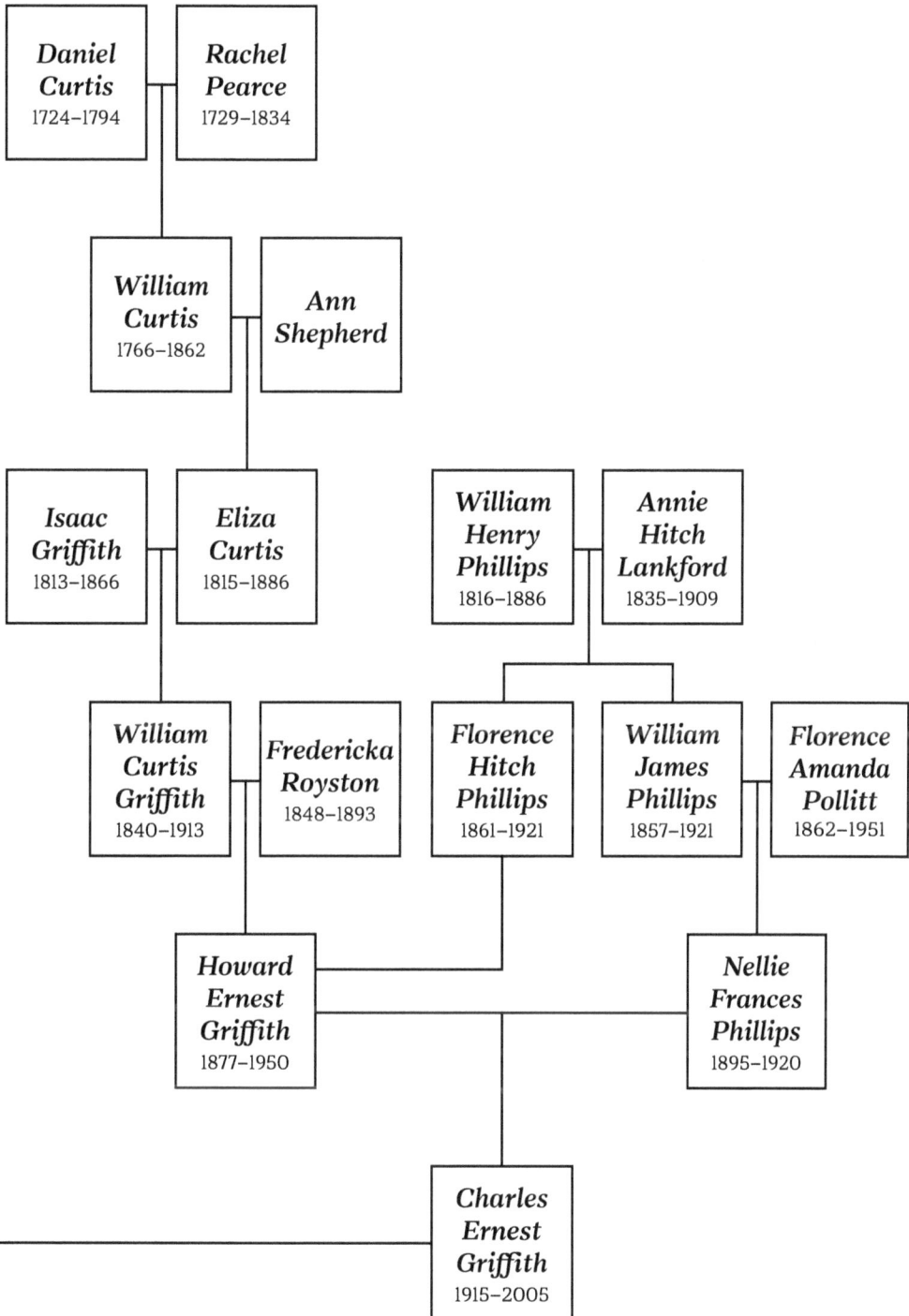

```
┌─────────────┬─────────────┐
│   Daniel    │   Rachel    │
│   Curtis    │   Pearce    │
│  1724–1794  │  1729–1834  │
└─────────────┴─────────────┘
        │
┌─────────────┬─────────────┐
│   William   │     Ann     │
│   Curtis    │  Shepherd   │
│  1766–1862  │             │
└─────────────┴─────────────┘
        │
┌─────────────┬─────────────┐     ┌─────────────┬─────────────┐
│    Isaac    │    Eliza    │     │   William   │    Annie    │
│  Griffith   │   Curtis    │     │    Henry    │    Hitch    │
│  1813–1866  │  1815–1886  │     │  Phillips   │  Lankford   │
└─────────────┴─────────────┘     │  1816–1886  │  1835–1909  │
        │                         └─────────────┴─────────────┘
                                          │
┌─────────────┬─────────────┐     ┌─────────────┬─────────────┬─────────────┐
│   William   │ Fredericka  │     │  Florence   │   William   │  Florence   │
│   Curtis    │  Royston    │     │    Hitch    │    James    │   Amanda    │
│  Griffith   │  1848–1893  │     │  Phillips   │  Phillips   │  Pollitt    │
│  1840–1913  │             │     │  1861–1921  │  1857–1921  │  1862–1951  │
└─────────────┴─────────────┘     └─────────────┴─────────────┴─────────────┘
        │                                                │
    ┌─────────────┐                              ┌─────────────┐
    │   Howard    │                              │   Nellie    │
    │   Ernest    │                              │   Frances   │
    │  Griffith   │──────────────────────────────│  Phillips   │
    │  1877–1950  │                              │  1895–1920  │
    └─────────────┘                              └─────────────┘
                            │
                    ┌─────────────┐
────────────────────│   Charles   │
                    │   Ernest    │
                    │  Griffith   │
                    │  1915–2005  │
                    └─────────────┘
```

Messrs. Editors:

I read with much interest the record of the Griffith family in a recent issue of the Baltimore SUN which, I understand, was prepared by you. I suppose that I come in somewhere, and have wondered where, or whether in your investigation anything was seen which would give me some light on my descent. My father's name was Isaac Griffith. He married Eliza Curtis, daughter of William Curtis, who lived on My Lady's Manor, in Baltimore county, and died at the age of 96. He told me he was in Annapolis when Washington resigned his commission. Our branch of the family, I think, came from Alexandria, Va. My grandfather, I have heard, was a Quaker. My father was a Methodist and lived and died in Baltimore county. I am now in my sixty-sixth year; am a minister of the Baltimore Conference. I have often been asked if I were related to Rev. Alfred Griffith, whose genealogy you give in THE SUN. I have mentioned nearly all I know on the subject. My father had a sister whose first name was Naomi. She died in Baltimore many years ago. An old lady whose daughter married a Mr. Scarborough, who lived for many years on Pennsylvania avenue, Baltimore, was a cousin of my father, and she told me about the genealogical tree, and about our side of the family coming from Alexandria, Va. If you have any information, helpful to me, may I solicit a line or two from you in regard thereto? I will be very much obliged. Glad to note the good work you are doing.

W. C. G.

[It was impossible to mention all the Griffith connections in our article. If our correspondent will write to Mrs. Romulus R. Griffith, 1529 McCulloh street, Baltimore, he can secure the information he asks.]

————

Baltimore Sun, *Feb. 19, 1905, p. 8.*

Introduction

IN FEBRUARY 1905, the *Baltimore Sun* published a long article about the history of the Griffith family in Maryland, tracking more than a thousand descendants of some of the original Griffith immigrants (although, as it turned out, none that were our ancestors). William Curtis Griffith wrote the letter to the editor shown on the facing page, dropping some hints that would be used more than a century later when this history of our Griffith family was written.

```
        ┌─────────────────┐
        │     August      │
        │     Günther     │
        │    1832–1908    │
        └────────┬────────┘
                 │
   ┌─────────────┴───┐     ┌─────────────────┐
   │     Richard     │     │     Amalie      │
   │     Julius      │     │     Terese      │
   │     Rudolph     ├─────┤    Stromeyer    │
   │    Guenther     │     │    1883–1959    │
   │    1872–1953    │     │                 │
   └─────────────────┘     └─────────────────┘
            ┌────────────┴────────────┐
   ┌────────┴────────┐       ┌─────────┴───────┐
   │   Richard J.    │       │     Amalie      │
   │  Guenther, Jr.  │       │     Louise      │
   │    1911–1999    │       │    Guenther     │
   └─────────────────┘       │    1914–2000    │
                             └─────────────────┘
```

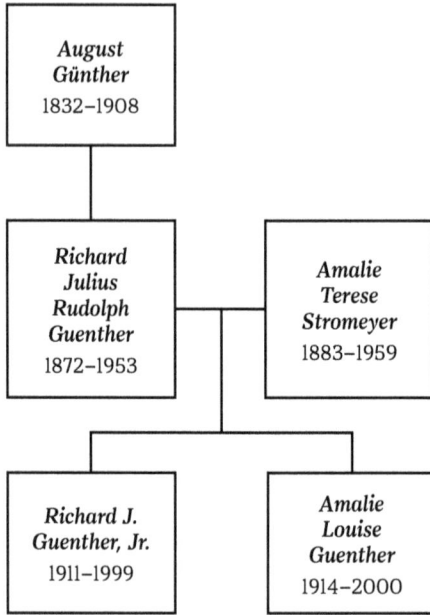

Descendants of August Günther (Guenther)

Guenther

August Günther (Guenther)
January 28, 1832–July 6, 1908

August lived in Gera, Germany, at Schulstrasse No. 18. He was very involved in the founding of an athletic club in Gera in 1880, now known as TSV 1880 Gera-Zwotzen e.V. (See www.tsv1880gera.de.) An article about the club, found in the archives at Piney Point, appears in Exhibit 1, which has been translated and is shown in Exhibit 2.

The article notes that August "joined our gymnastics society as a 19-year-old cloth-maker's journeyman" on April 23, 1851. He created a singing group, was active in gymnastics, and was involved with several building drives.

August had at least two relatives in Gera in 1932: Alfred Guenther (living at Schmelzhuetten Strasse 14, Gera, Germany) and Walter Guenther (living in Possneck, about 37 km from Gera). The 1932 Christmas Card List of R. J. and Amalie Guenther shows a number of addresses with names, many of which are of other relatives discussed in this book. (See Exhibit 3.)

We don't know the name of August's wife, but there is a photo of
the couple, which was taken in Gera in 1890.

August Guenther and wife. Gera, Germany, 1890.

Richard Julius Rudolph Guenther
August 9, 1872–November 30, 1953

August and his wife had at least one son, Richard Julius Rudolph Guenther, who was born in Gera on August 9, 1872. At age 19, Richard left for the United States on the ship *Russia*, departing from Hamburg, Germany, and arriving in New York on September 28, 1891. He carried with him both a letter from his father and a book. Note the spelling of his name on the book, with the German "ü." The ship's passenger list, from the National Archives, is shown in Exhibit 4.

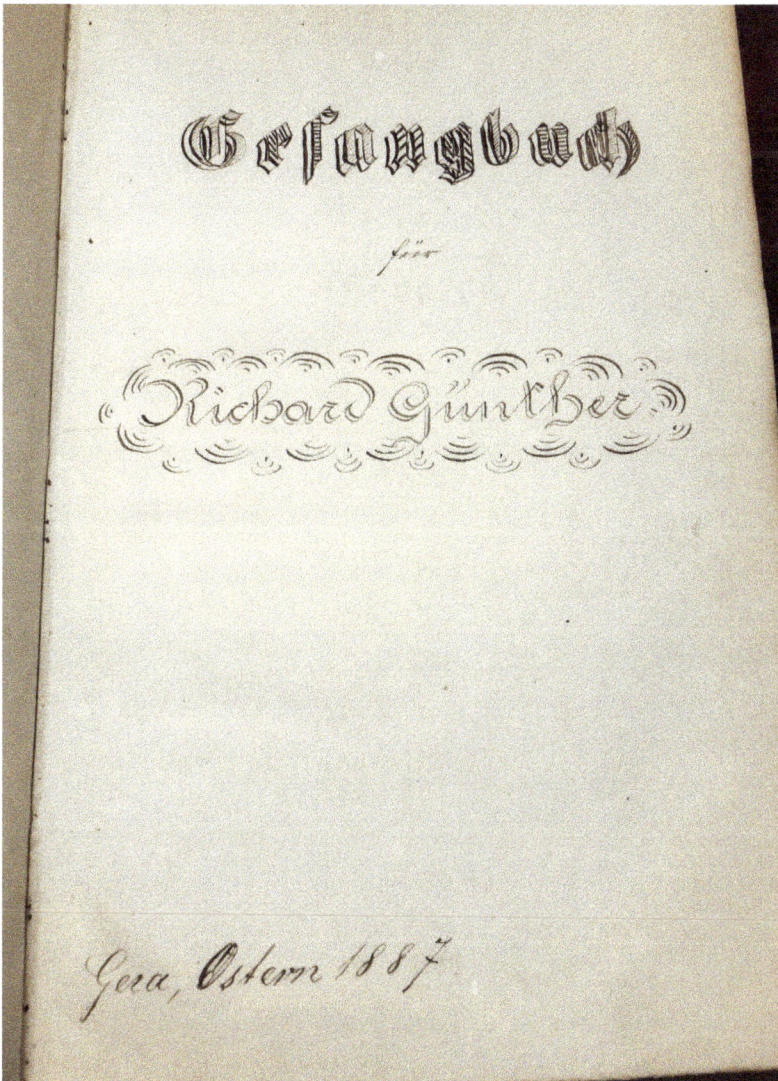

Richard's book, in the archives at Piney Point.

He had his picture taken in August 1891, right before he left Germany.

Richard Guenther, August 1891.

On June 29, 1901, Richard married Hermine (Schlessinger) Farchmin, who had three young daughters from her first marriage. Hermine was also from Gera and had arrived in New York on July 26, 1886. She died on March 16, 1905, only a few years after she and Richard married. They had no children together. She is buried at the Linden Hill Methodist Cemetery in Ridgewood, Queens, in Lot C, No. 68. This was when the Guenther plot was purchased; in addition to Hermine and Richard, Amalie Terese (Stromeyer) Guenther, Anna (Harberger) Stromeyer, and Walter Stromeyer are buried there.

GUENTHER—On Thursday, 16th, HERMINE GUENTHER, beloved wife and mother, entered into heavenly rest.
The funeral will take place on Sunday, the 19th inst., from the German Methodist Episcopal Church, 346 Fortieth et., near Ninth av, New York City, at 1:30 P.M. Richard Guenther, husband; Anna, Lisa and Elsa Farchmin, children. Kindly omit flowers.   17-3

Hermine Guenther Obituary. **Brooklyn Daily Eagle**
(Brooklyn, N.Y.), Sat., March 18, 1905, p. 20.

Richard became a naturalized U.S. citizen on February 24, 1899. (See Exhibit 5.) He returned to Germany numerous times, and his name can be found on multiple passport applications and travel documents as a "merchant" traveling between the United States and Germany. A passport application appears in Exhibit 6.

Hermine's daughters—Anna, Lisa, and Elsa Farchmin—remained in touch with Richard, and later, with Richard and his second wife, Amalie. Anna became a nurse, and is found on the 1905 Census at a nursing school in New York City. Lisa, the second daughter (b. 1885), married Adolph Vogt in 1908 and moved to Montclair, N.J. Adolph Vogt was the comptroller for U.S. Steel. He and Lisa (Farchmin) Vogt had three children – Julia, John, and Virginia. Virginia married Walker Woods Stevenson and lived in Princeton. One of Walker's and Virginia's daughters, Sharon Stevenson, married a Charles Griffith and now

Richard Guenther

lives in Pound Ridge! Hermine's third daughter, Elsa Farchmin, was living with Richard Guenther in the 1910 census, and was a teacher. In 1914, Elsa married George Edward Bush and also moved to Montclair.

On September 13, 1910, Richard married Amalie Terese Stromeyer, the daughter of William Stromeyer and Balbina Agatha Johner. The marriage was duly recorded in the Episcopal Diocese of New York's records for Trinity Church.

Initially, they lived at 1008 Trinity Avenue, which was Amalie's family home. Later, they moved to Mount Vernon. In both the 1920 and 1930 censuses, they are living at 58 North Columbus Avenue; in the 1940 census, they are living at 79th Street in Queens. Richard's occupation is listed as salesman, silks and textile merchant.

Richard Guenther.

Amalie Terese Stromeyer Guenther.

Their children were Richard Julius Guenther Jr., born on November 7, 1911, and Amalie Louise Guenther, born on December 9, 1914.

Amalie Guenther with Amalie and Richard Jr.

Amalie and Richard Jr.

Richard "R. J." Guenther died on November 30, 1953, and Amalie Terese Stromeyer Guenther died on January 2, 1959. Richard and Amalie are buried in the Guenther plot at Linden Hill Cemetery.

Richard Julius Guenther Jr.
November 7, 1911–February 5, 1999

Richard ("Uncle Dick") was born on November 7, 1911. He attended the Massachusetts Institute of Technology and graduated from New York University with a degree in chemical engineering. He was married, first, to Edith, with whom he had two children, Richard W. and Carol. Richard married, second, June Dorothy Soper, with whom he had a daughter, Laurie. His last marriage was to Lucille Walther. Richard's daughter Carol later married Gerald W. Petz, and they had several children.

Uncle Dick and June.

Seated on sofa, back row, left to right: Charles E. Griffith (Alan on lap), Richard Guenther, Amalie Guenther, Edith (Carol on lap);
front row: *Amalie Griffith (Chuck on lap) and Richard Guenther Jr. (ca. 1943).*

Amalie Louise Guenther
December 9, 1914–February 27, 2000

Amalie ("Gammy") was born on December 9, 1914, when her family lived at 58 N. Columbus Avenue in Mt. Vernon, New York. As a young girl, she went to summer camp in Maine.

Amalie, age 12, with her father, Richard.

Amalie went to Teachers College, Columbia University, which included some time student teaching at the New College Community Nursery School in North Carolina.

Amalie, at right, student teaching in 1934.

On September 16, 1936, she married Charles Ernest Griffith in New York City.

```
                    ┌──────────┬──────────┐
                    │   Karl   │          │
                    │  Joseph  │  Maria   │
                    │ Stromeyer│  Nischl  │
                    └──────────┴──────────┘
                          │
                    ┌──────────┬──────────┐
                    │  Franz   │          │
                    │  Joseph  │ Marianne │
                    │ Stromeyer│   West   │
                    │1805–1848 │          │
                    └──────────┴──────────┘
```

| Balbina Agatha Johner 1848–1889 | William Alexander Stromeyer 1844–1906 | Amalie Sophie Stromeyer 1842–1928 | Evelina Maria Stromeyer | Ida Stromeyer | Anna Stromeyer |

Anna Harberger 1870–1935

| Maria Ida Stromeyer 1868–1954 | Wilhelm Stromeyer 1875–1879 | William Theodore Stromeyer 1880–1911 | Amalie Terese Stromeyer 1883–1959 | Alfred Stromeyer 1886–1888 |

| Charles Francis Stromeyer 1872–1924 | Joseph Safron Stromeyer 1877–1887 | Richard Stromeyer 1881–1882 | Elizabeth Martha (Elsie) Stromeyer 1885–1961 |

| Walther Stromeyer 1893–1894 | Walter Hermann Stromeyer 1894–1947 | Victor Stromeyer 1897–1898 |

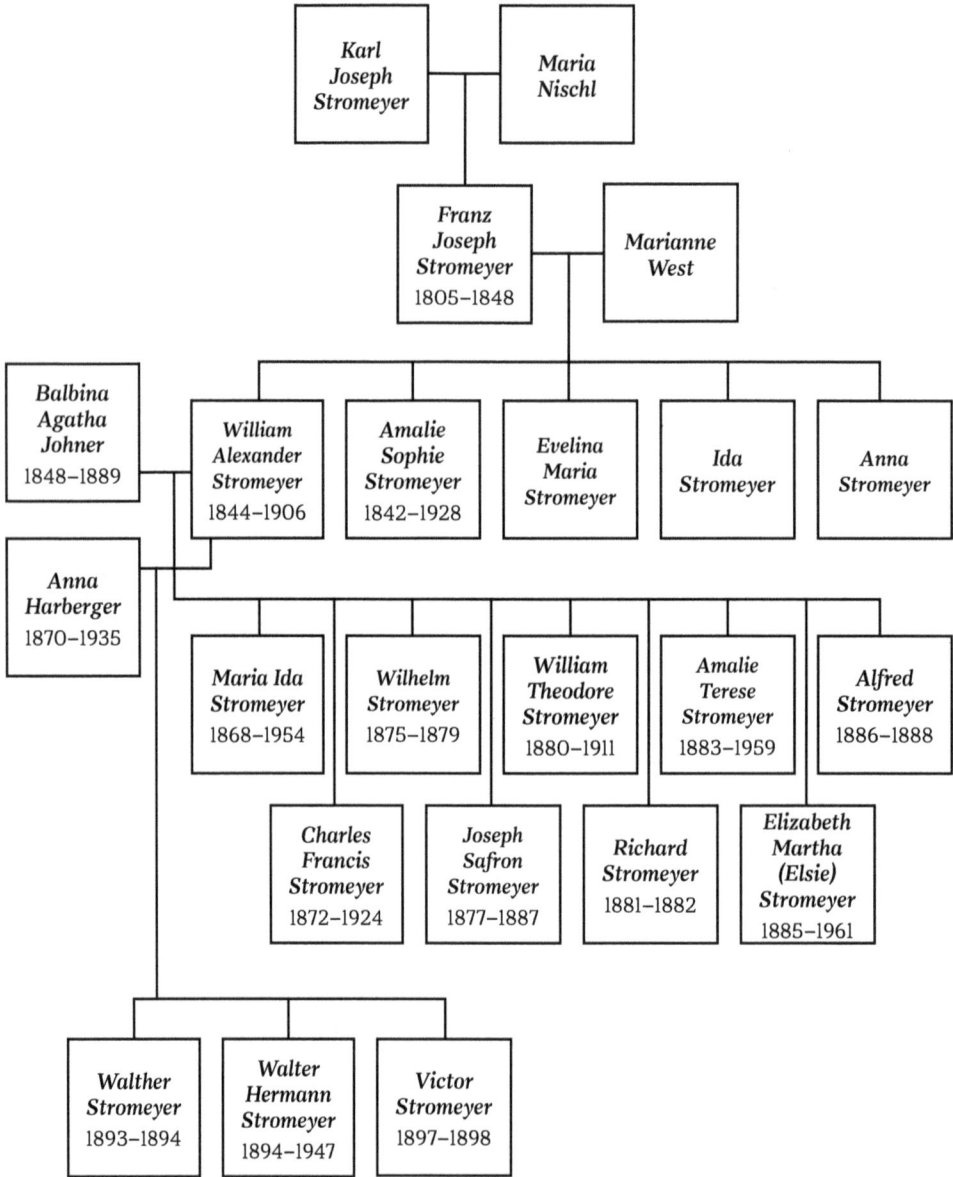

Descendants of Karl Joseph Stromeyer and Maria Nischl

Stromeyer

GERALD PETZ, another genealogist in the family, completed the family tree (Exhibit 7), which traces the Stromeyers back until the 1600s in Germany. He suggests that we may be related to Friedrich Stromeyer, who discovered cadmium in 1817. Documented family history, however, begins with Karl Joseph Stromeyer and Maria Nischl, the parents of Franz Stromeyer.

Franz Joseph Stromeyer
August 9, 1805–December 18, 1848

Wikipedia described Franz as a German publisher, journalist, and revolutionary. He was arrested several times, particularly in 1832 after speaking at the Hambach Festival, a national democratic festival in Germany. Fleeing warrants for his arrest, he lived for a time in London beginning in 1837, where he met and married Marianne West in St. Mary, Islington, in a Church of England ceremony after the banns were published three times. (See Exhibit 8.) The 1841 England Census lists them as living in Putney, England, where Franz is listed as a "Professor of German."

The couple had five children: Amalie Sophie, William Alexander, Evelina Maria, Ida, and Anna. The children were born in France, Germany, and Switzerland; the family moved frequently as Franz was expelled from one country after another for his socialist activities. All the children were baptized in a Lutheran church in Baden, Germany, where they lived for a short time. Wikipedia suggests he was also involved in various intelligence and counter-intelligence operations.

According to a letter from the Ursuline Archives in Australia detailing Amalie's life, Franz and Marianne both died while the children were very young; the children went to live with various relatives.

He died in Constance, Switzerland.

Amalie Sophie Stromeyer
October 18, 1842–July 14, 1928

The oldest child of Franz and Marianne, Amalie lived a fascinating life. Born in Citteaux, France, she was raised by an uncle after her parents' deaths, and went to Duderstadt, Germany, to study for the examination required to be a public teacher. While there, she converted to Catholicism and, after a few years as a tutor in Brussels, entered the Order of St. Ursula, becoming an Ursuline nun at the age of 18. On May 24, 1882, she left Greenwich, England, with nine other Ursuline nuns and two postulants, for Armidale in New South Wales, Australia, to establish a convent and a new day and boarding school for Catholic girls (and later, boys). The journey took fourteen weeks. Her name, along with the other nuns, is now on the Welcome Wall at the Australian National Maritime Museum in Sydney, Australia. (See Exhibit 9 for the story from the December, 2010 edition of *Signals*, the magazine of the Australian National Maritime Museum.)

The Welcome Wall in Sydney, Australia.

Amalie Stromeyer's name as it appears on the Welcome Wall.

Amelia took the name Sister Cecilia as a nun when she joined the order in Germany. Her journeys began when, in May 1873, Chancellor Bismarck enacted a series of laws in Germany that required all teaching religious orders to be dissolved or expelled from the territories of the new German empire and their property confiscated, with education passing to the control of the state. Thus, the Ursulines left for England in 1877, where they started a new school in Greenwich. It was from there that the group of twelve volunteered to sail for Australia on the *Duchess of Edinburgh*, a clipper ship. Once in Australia, they established the "High School for Young Ladies," which became the very well-known College of St. Ursula in Armidale, which at that time was a very rural and undeveloped area. The school continued until the mid-1970s, when it merged with a nearby school and moved. The nuns lived at the convent until 2011.

A history of the Order of St. Ursula in Australia reported that "Sister Cecilia Stromeyer was so fluent in French that when she taught this subject in the high school many believe[d] she was of French nationality rather than German." She also taught music and was the "Mistress of Studies" and the "Mistress of Boarders" at different times. In 1918, she was celebrated for her fifty years of service to the Order. (See Exhibit 10.)

She was the last of the original founders of the convent to die, and she was buried in the nun's section in Armidale Catholic Cemetery. (See Exhibit 11.)

William Alexander Stromeyer
July 14, 1844–December 2, 1906

William was born in Emmishofer, Switzerland. Family legend is that he swam across Lake Constance to escape imprisonment as a Socialist. His father died when he was very young, and, at age 21, William immigrated to New York, arriving on February 27, 1866 on the SS *Hermann*.

Also on the same ship was Balbina Johner, who was 18 years old and traveling without any family. It is unknown if she had already known William or if she met him on board, but they married on June 3, 1866, in the First German Presbyterian Church on Rivington Street in New York, New York.

William was naturalized on October 19, 1871. He was an upholsterer and interior designer and operated a furniture store at 4 E. 9th Street in New York. His letterhead announced that Stromeyer carried "Fine Furniture and Upholstery."

Balbina and William had nine children: Maria "Ida" (b. 1868), Charles Francis (b. 1872), Wilhelm (b. 1875), Joseph Safron (b. 1877), William Theodore (b. 1880), Richard (b. 1881), Amalie Terese (b. 1883), Elizabeth Martha (b. 1885), and Alfred J. (b. 1886).

Children of Balbina and William, left to right: Amalie, William, Maria "Ida," Charles, and Elizabeth ("Elsie") Stromeyer, most probably ca. 1890.

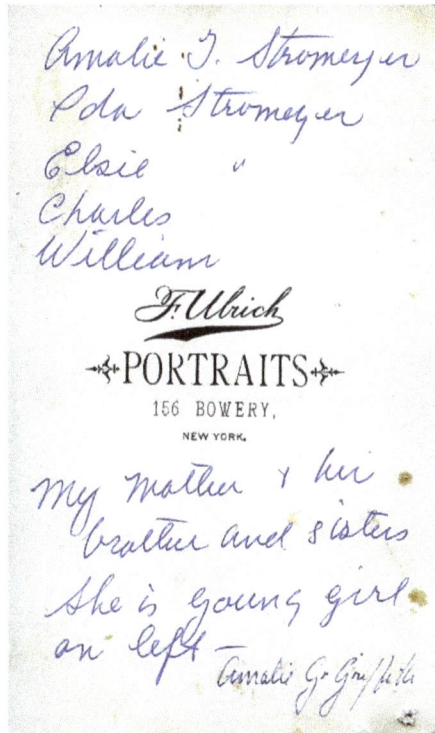

Amalie Griffith's handwritten note on the back of the photo of the children.

Wilhelm died in 1879 (age 4), Richard died in 1882 (age 1), Joseph died in 1887 (age 10), and Alfred died in 1888 (age 1); the four young boys are buried with their father and mother at St. Michael's Cemetery in Queens. The headstone is written entirely in German.

Balbina died in 1889. William married, second, Anna Harberger (1870–April 29, 1935), a nurse or nanny for the family, and the couple had three children: Walther (b. 1893), Walter Hermann (b. 1894), and Victor (b. 1897). Walther and Victor also died young and are buried with their father.

William lived at 1008 Trinity Avenue in the Bronx and died there on December 2, 1906, of typhoid fever. After his death, Anna and Walter continued to live there.

William and Balbina's daughter Maria "Ida" (December 30, 1868–August 19, 1954) married Henry Peter Botty (January 28, 1872–1942) in 1895. They are buried in the Botty family plot in Woodlawn Cemetery. They did not have any children. Henry Botty may have been the connection between the Stromeyer family and the Guenthers. A lawyer, Henry Botty was a witness, along with Adolph Vogt, to Hermine Guenther's will in 1904, testifying that he had been a family friend. Henry Botty was also one of the executors and witnesses to William Stromeyer's will in 1906.

Charles Francis (1872–September 4, 1924) became an interior designer, as his father had done. Charles married Emma Clara Schaefer (1877–1937); they had four children. Charles took his own life by eating a peach that he had filled with poison.

William Theodore (1880–1911) attended Columbia College (which became Columbia University in 1896), became an electrical engineer, and then moved to Dallas, Texas, where, in 1905, he married Lillian Genavive McDonald. They then moved to Brownwood, Texas, in West Texas. William was a general manager for the West Texas Telephone Company (which later became one of the companies that merged to become AT&T). He and Lillian had two children, William Alexander and Irene. William Theadore's body was returned to New York City for burial in the family plot in St. Michael's Cemetery, Queens. In an interesting footnote, Lillian was the favorite niece of William Johnson McDonald, who died in 1926, leaving a fortune to the University of Texas to establish the McDonald Observatory. Young William and Irene also inherited a part of the fortune.

Elizabeth Martha ("Elsie") (1885–February 15, 1961) married Percival Arnold Huerstel (April 28, 1878–December 21, 1954). They had two children, Percival Arnold Huerstel Jr. and Constance. Constance married Howard Bailey Ferris; they had two children, Barbara and Charles.

Amalie Terese, William and Balbina's second youngest daughter, married Richard Guenther.

Walter Stromeyer, William and Anna's son, served in World War I in the Navy, starting as a seaman and later becoming an ensign. He died on September 29, 1947, and is buried in the Guenther plot at Linden Hill Cemetery, as is his mother, who had died in 1935.

From left (back row): *Richard Guenther, Howard Ferris, Amalie Guenther, Elizabeth Huerstel, Amalie Griffith, Percy Huerstel, and Constance Ferris (with Barbara Ferris in her arms).*
Front row: *Chuck and Alan Griffith and Charles Ferris.*

```
                  ┌─────────────┐   ┌─────────────┐
                  │   Daniel    │   │   Rachel    │
                  │   Curtis    │───│   Pearce    │
                  │  1724–1794  │   │             │
                  └─────────────┘   └─────────────┘
                        ┌─────────────┐   ┌─────────────┐
                        │  William    │   │    Ann      │
                        │  Curtis     │───│  Shepherd   │
                        │  1766–1862  │   │             │
                        └─────────────┘   └─────────────┘
```

| Rachel Curtis 1794–1880 | John Shepherd Curtis 1795–1871 | Thomas Curtis 1799–1869 | Levi Curtis 1801–1890 | Sarah Curtis 1803–1878 |
| William Curtis 1805–1876 | Eli Curtis 1807–1876 | Ann Curtis 1809–1880 | Ira Curtis 1811–1880 | Eliza Curtis 1815–1886 |

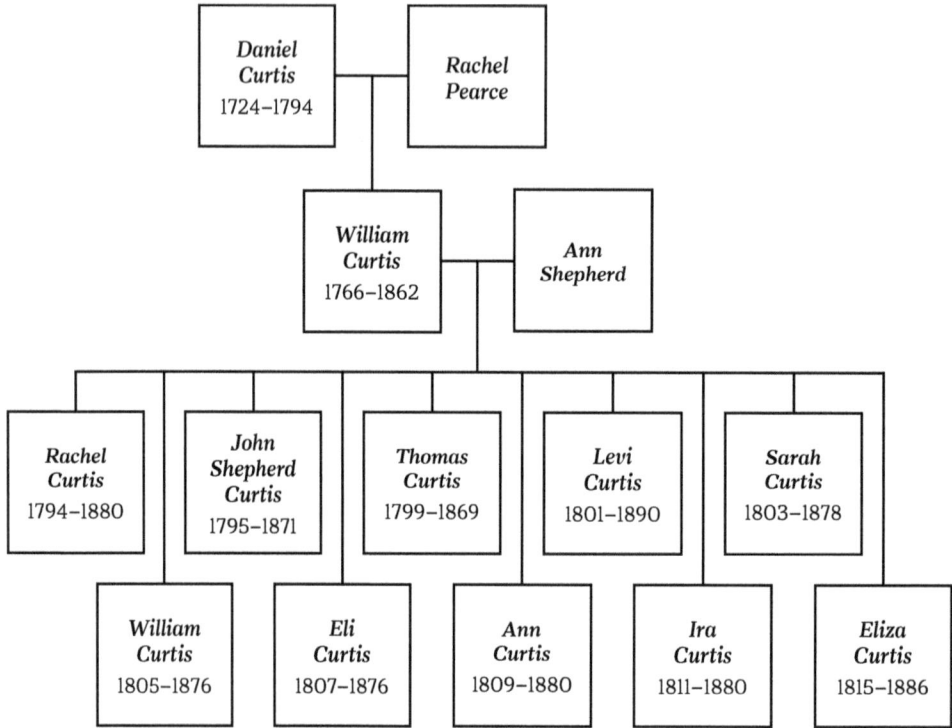

Descendants of Daniel Curtis and Rachel Pearce

Curtis

Daniel Curtis
July 21, 1724–1794

Daniel Curtis was born in England, baptized in the Church of England in London. He was transported to the colonies as a convict in 1750; he landed in Maryland, marrying Rachel Pearce on November 5, 1758. They had a number of children, including William Curtis, born in 1766 in My Lady's Manor.

My Lady's Manor is an area of Harford and Baltimore Counties, approximately 10,000 acres in size, that has a colorful history, originating as an inheritance from Lord Baltimore to his daughter, which was then deeded to Thomas Brerewood, who had fled England deep in debt. He became quite successful, developing and leasing the land. Maryland's legislature confiscated My Lady's Manor during the Revolutionary War. In 1782, the new state of Maryland sold the lands to various families, most of whom had been Brerewood's tenants. The town of Monkton is the largest town in My Lady's Manor.

Daniel prospered in Baltimore County, becoming the overseer of roads. His wife, Rachel, was the daughter of William Pearce, also one of the founders of My Lady's Manor.

William Curtis
1766–March 2, 1862

William Curtis married Ann Shepherd, also from an original My Lady's Manor family. They had ten children:

Rachel Curtis	1794–1880
John Shepherd Curtis	1795–1871
Thomas Curtis	1799–1869
Levi Curtis	1801–1890
Sarah Curtis	1803–1878
William Curtis	1805–1876
Eli Curtis	1807–1876
Ann Curtis	1809–1880
Ira Curtis	1811–1880
Eliza Curtis	1815–1886

All of the children were baptized at Saint James Protestant Episcopal Church, in Monkton, Maryland, and many are buried there with their families. William, and later Levi and Eli, were on the vestry of the church for several terms, and the church records contain many references to their contributions. Several of the children married into prominent My Lady's Manor families, including Rachel, who married Daniel Sparks.

The elder William was very successful as a farmer, owning a significant amount of land in the 10th District, which is where My Lady's Manor is located. He lived to be 96 years old. William and Ann do not appear to be buried at St. James, which is unusual given their involvement with the Parish. Many of their sons, however, are buried in the cemetery.

In William's will he left his property, including several slaves, horses, "bed and bedding," cows, and cash bequests amongst his many children. However, his daughter Eliza's only bequest was:

> I will and bequest unto my daughter Eliza Griffith Five
> Hundred Dollars and whereas her husband stands
> indebted to me in the sum of Six Hundred and Forty-

nine dollars and fifty cents, I order said demise be deducted from said debt.

Eliza contested the will, bringing an action against her brothers to compel payment of the bequest. Her son, William Curtis Griffith, represented her; the matter was resolved by settlement.

Eliza Griffith, by her next friend, vs. John S. Curtis and Wm. Curtis, Jr., executors of Wm Curtis, deceased. Bill filed to compel payment of a legacy of $500 to Eliza Griffith by the defendants, executors of Wm. Curtis, deceased. Bill dismissed. Messrs. Geary and Griffith for complainant; Messrs. Boarman and Gittings for defendants.

Baltimore Sun, *June 24, 1865, p. 4.*

Eliza Curtis married Isaac Griffith of My Lady's Manor on April 9, 1839.

MARRIED.

On the 28th ult., by the Rev. Mr. Smith, Mr. Wm. Dorsey to Miss Margaret T. Martain, all of this city.

On the 9th inst., by the Rev. Mr. Tippet, Mr. Isaac Griffith to Miss Eliza Curtis, both of My Lady's Manor, Baltimore county, Md.

On the 16th inst., by the Rev. Dr. Roberts, James Collines to Miss Aberiller Man, all of this city.

At Galena, Illinois, on the 21st ult., by the Rev. Mr. Kent, Mr. Gerhart H. Mars to Miss Charlotte Schwatka, formerly of Baltimore, Md., youngest daughter of August Schwatka.

Baltimore Sun, *April 16, 1839.*

```
                    ┌──────────┬──────────┐
                    │  Isaac   │  Eliza   │
                    │ Griffith │  Curtis  │
                    │1813–1866 │1815–1886 │
                    └──────────┴──────────┘
```

| John Griffith 1841–1841 | John James Griffith 1843–1893 | Margaret Ann Griffith 1843–1868 | Thomas Alfred Griffith 1844–1853 | Winfield Scott Griffith 1848–1900 | Spencer Vinton Griffith 1853–1868 |

| Julia Belle Harbaugh 1862–1931 | William Curtis Griffith 1840–1913 | Fredericka Royston 1848–1893 | | George Milton Griffith 1846–1864 | Isaac Newton Griffith 1852–1854 | Franklin Griffith 1858–1860 |

| Ruth E. Griffith 1897–1971 | Albert Spencer Griffith 1869–1928 | Howard Ernest Griffith 1877–1950 | Nellie Frances Phillips 1895–1920 |

| Charles Ernest Griffith 1915–2005 |

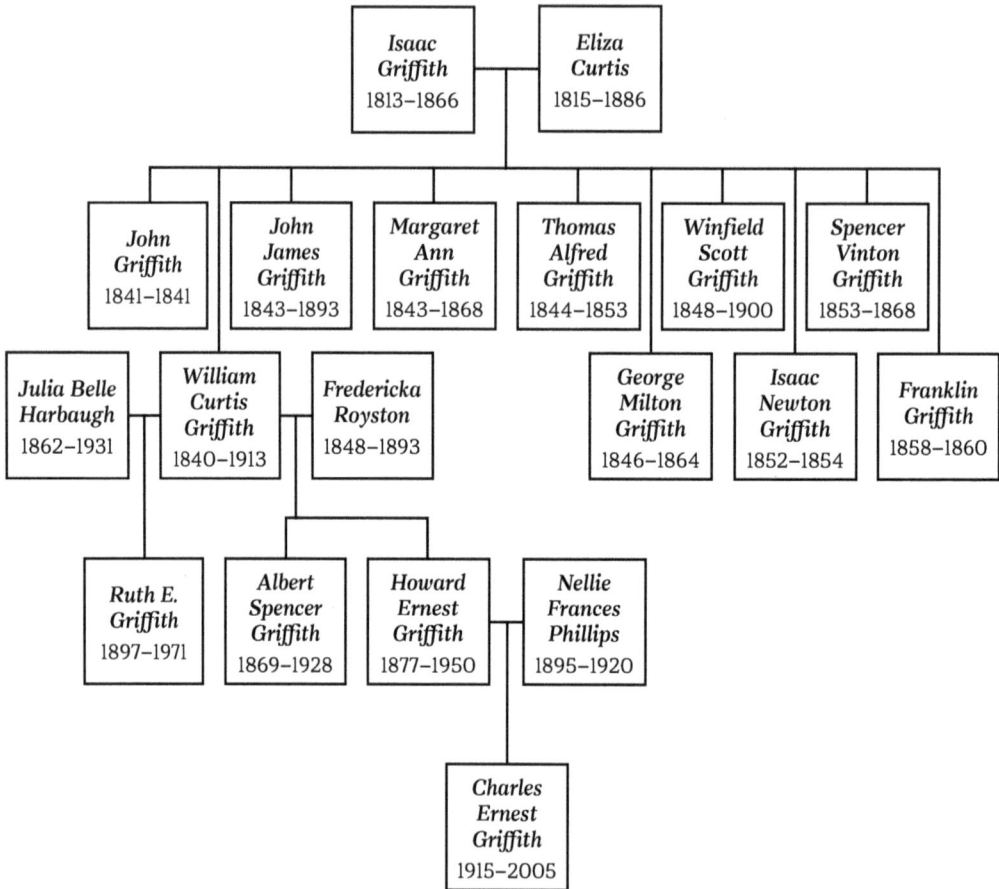

Descendants of Isaac Griffith and Eliza Curtis

Griffith

Isaac Griffith
August 1813–October 21, 1866

The first documented Griffith is Isaac Griffith, born in My Lady's Manor, Baltimore County, in August 1813. Because of his connection to My Lady's Manor, it is possible to make some guesses about Isaac's heritage.

It is likely that Isaac was descended from Howell Griffith, who arrived in Philadelphia, Pennsylvania, from Wales sometime before 1689, having fled persecution as a Quaker. Howell had been committed to jail in Carnarthshire, Wales, in June 1684. The family moved to Bucks County; as Quakers, the family's history is well documented in early Quaker records.

Howell's oldest son, Abraham, was born in Wales in 1680. Abraham and his wife, Hannah Lester, are buried at the Richland Friends Meeting Burial Ground in Quakertown, Bucks County. Their oldest son was Isaac Griffith, born in Richland, Pennsylvania, in 1720. Isaac married Ann Burson in 1744, and, in 1769, the couple moved to the My Lady's Manor area of Maryland where they joined the Gunpowder Monthly Meeting. The Gunpowder Monthly Meeting House is in Sparks, in My Lady's Manor.

Isaac and Ann had several children. In 1769, when they moved to My Lady's Manor, the children were identified as: Abraham, Hannah, Mary, Ann, Sarah, Joseph, Martha, Elizabeth, Isaac, John, and James. They later moved to Fairfax, Virginia. However, when Ann Burson died, Isaac remarried, and was promptly in trouble with the

Quakers because he "married outside the good order" by marrying the widow of his wife's brother, also named Ann Burson. As a result, the Fairfax Quaker Monthly Meeting refused to approve the marriage.[1] Isaac sought reinstatement to the Fairfax Meeting, at which he was ultimately successful. Following his reinstatement, he returned to Gunpowder and was accepted there on December 22, 1781:

> Twenty-second of Ninth month, 1781, Isaac Griffith's paper condemning his misconduct in marrying his former wife's brother's wife was read and was satisfactory. The case was on hand for two years.

Several of Isaac's children remained in Fairfax, while some remained in Gunpowder, and he was traveling back and forth:

> Isaac Griffith having come to live on the verge of this meeting hath returned the Certificate we gave him to Fairfax Monthly Meeting in Virginia dated 24th day of the 11th month of 1782 which by this meeting received.

However, by April 30, 1803, he was in trouble with the Fairfax meeting again:

> On 30 April 1803 hath frequently neglected attendance of our religious meetings, hath frequented games and other places of diversion, hath been concerned with horseracing and made use of unbecoming language, has removed within the verge of Fairfax Meeting. On 26 November 1803 had been located and charges presented against him in Fairfax Monthly Meeting.

He gave a written apology in January 1804. He died in 1866; his burial location is not known.

---

1   The Religious Society of Friends, or Quakers, met monthly and kept extensive minutes of these meetings. The Quakers did not separate secular and religious life, so the minutes contain comprehensive references to activities. The Quaker minutes are available through numerous sources, including online databases and reference manuals.

Isaac's oldest child, Abraham, married Mary Moore on April 3, 1771. Mary died on September 13, 1784. Abraham and Mary had the following children, recorded in the Gunpowder Monthly Meeting records: Ann, Reuben, Isaac, Miriam, and Sophia. After Mary's death, Abraham Griffith married Rachel Taylor on December 30, 1788, and they had four children: Thomas Taylor, Mary, Rachel, and Sarah.

Abraham died on May 26, 1800 and is buried at the Gunpowder Monthly Meeting House, as is his first wife, Mary Moore.

Another one of Isaac's children, Joseph, relocated from Gunpowder Falls to Belmont, Ohio, in 1808, after also being removed from the Quakers.

In addition to Joseph, several other of Isaac's children (including his own son, Isaac, born in 1764) and several of Abraham's children (including his son, also named Isaac, born August 25, 1776), left the Quakers and are no longer found in the records.

Given the large number of Griffiths in the Gunpowder/My Lady's Manor area from 1769 through 1814, and the prevalence of similar names, including James, when "our" Isaac Griffith was born, it is likely there was a connection. This speculation is further supported by the family history of one of Isaac's sons, Winfield Scott, who moved to Ohio to live with an uncle, as reported by Winfield's descendants.

The family Bible, from the Piney Point archives (excerpts attached as Exhibit 12) identifies Isaac's parents as James and Margaret. These are common names among the offspring of the original Isaac Griffith and Abraham Griffith, further suggesting a connection.

Isaac Griffith is first found on the census for 1840 in My Lady's Manor. When the 1850 census was taken, Isaac and Eliza were living on Stringtown Road, between Falls and Yeoho Roads, near Sparks, Maryland, also in the My Lady's Manor area. His occupation is listed as farmer; the house is listed on the Maryland Historical Trust as the "Glikin House" and is still standing today. It was part of the "Fair Play" manor, deeded to George Chilcoat in 1789, and purchased by Thomas Cole in 1838.

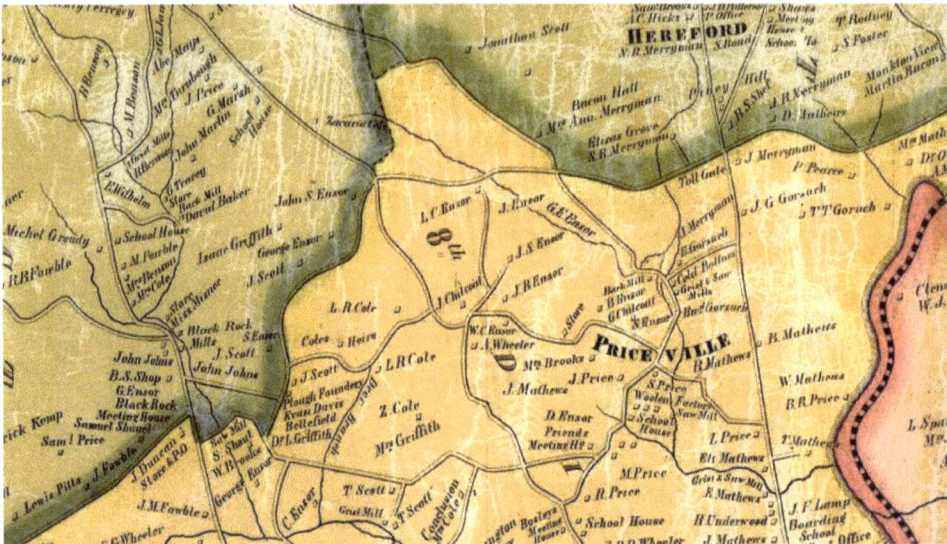

Taylor, Robert. Map of the city and county of Baltimore, Maryland.
Baltimore, 1857. Map. Retrieved from the Library of Congress.

Isaac and Eliza moved by 1857 to land near the Union House Post Office, in the 5th district of Baltimore County, which is outside of the My Lady's Manor area. The 1857 Map of Baltimore County shows that Isaac's land is very close to the land of a "Dr. L. Griffith" and Mrs. Griffith, although it is unclear how these individuals are related.

By 1862, Isaac had lost the farm, and, as noted earlier, was also in debt to his father-in-law.

A farm in the fifth district, containing 200 acres, and formerly owned by Isaac Griffith, was sold for taxes to day, by James W. Owngs, auctioneer, to Jacob Ellinger, for $250.

Baltimore Sun, *Dec. 10, 1862, p. 1.*

Isaac and Eliza moved to the city of Baltimore, to 142 East Monument Street, where they ran a hay market. Isaac died on October 21, 1866, and Eliza on February 7, 1886. Their burial locations are not known with certainty, but they are likely at the Mt. Carmel United Methodist Church in Parkton, Maryland (less than 5 miles from their former home on what is now Stringfellow Road). Although there are no burial records from that time period, and no identifiable headstones in the cemetery (many are weathered beyond reading), the death certificate for Eliza and the notices in the *Baltimore Sun* for Eliza and several of their children provide enough identifying information for this cemetery.

Isaac and Eliza had the following children:

William Curtis	January 19, 1840–April 27, 1913
John Griffith	March 24, 1841–December 15, 1841
John James	May 2, 1843 (twin)–February 7, 1893
Margaret Ann	May 2, 1843 (twin)–July 16, 1868
Thomas Alfred	December 26, 1844–August 25, 1853
George Milton	May 5, 1846–August 5, 1864
Winfield Scott	June 11, 1848–April 19, 1900
Isaac Newton	February 5, 1852–April 22, 1854
Spencer Vinton	May 9, 1853–January 3, 1868
Franklin	April 23, 1858–August 22, 1860

Five of these children died young. Margaret Ann and Spencer Vinton both died in 1868; John James committed suicide in 1893. (See Exhibit 13 for the obituary notices.)

Winfield Scott moved to Iowa and married Sarah Catherine Norris on July 15, 1884. They had one child, William Ersie Griffith, 1885–1935, who in turn had five children. Winfield went to Ohio to live with an uncle, and from there went on to Iowa. Ersie's granddaughter, in her family archives, notes that Winfield Scott left Baltimore because his father, Isaac, had become destitute during the Civil War, and Winfield went to live with an uncle's family in Ohio.

William Curtis, Margaret, John James, and Winfield Scott were all teachers.

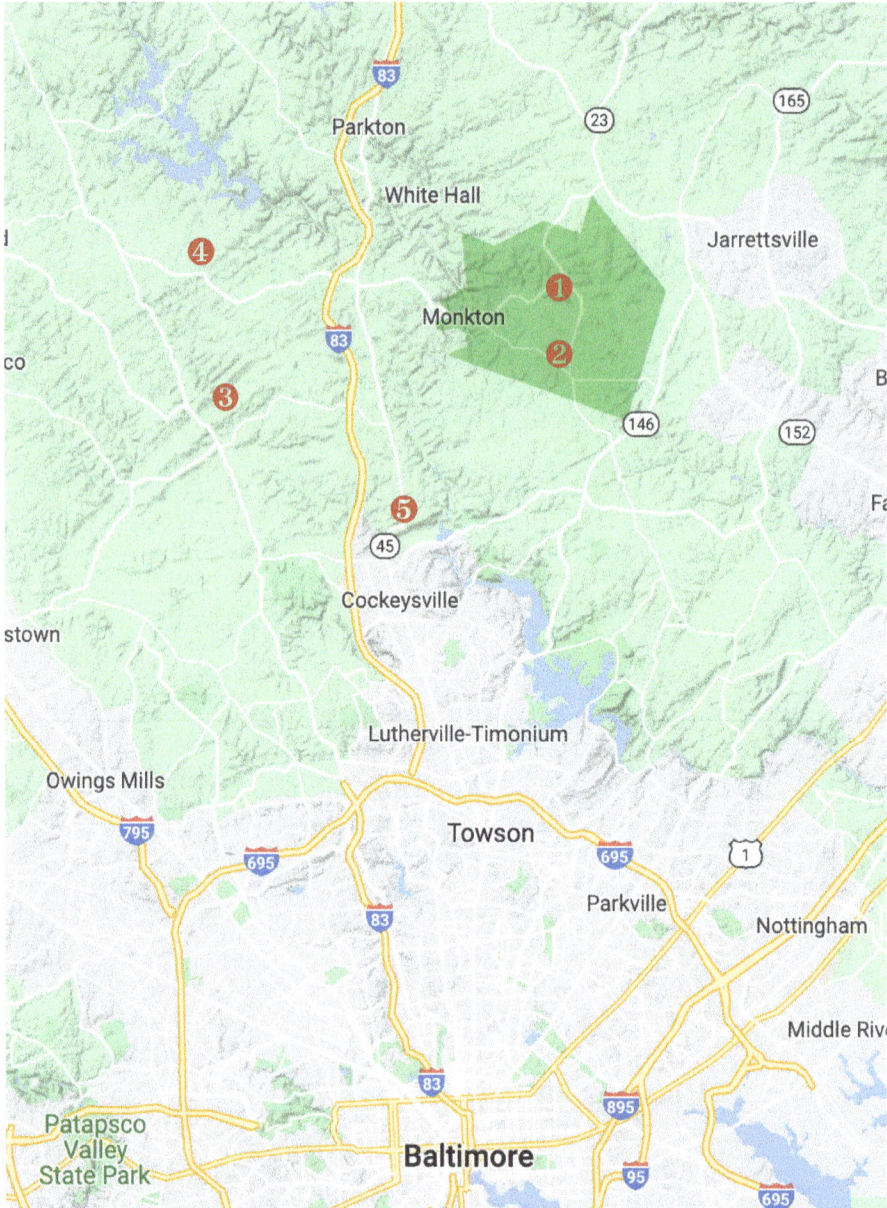

❶ *My Lady's Manor covers approximately 10,000 acres in and around Monkton.*

❷ *The Curtis Family lived in My Lady's Manor, and is buried at St. James Episcopal Church.*

❸ *Isaac Griffith and his family lived at the Griffith House from prior to 1850 until approximately 1862.*

❹ *Isaac Griffith and family are buried at Mt. Carmel United Methodist Church.*

❺ *William Curtis Griffith was a circuit preacher throughout the area, and is buried at the Historic Jessops Church in Sparks.*

Rev. William Curtis Griffith
January 19, 1840–April 27, 1913

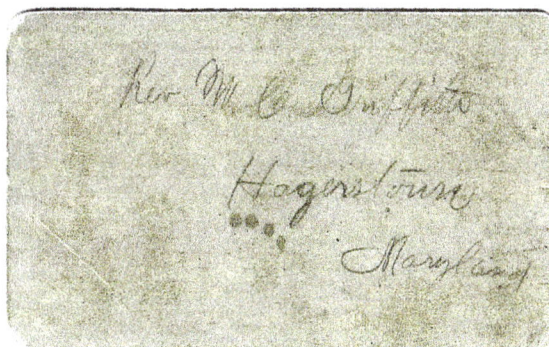

William Curtis Griffith.

William Curtis Griffith, the eldest child of Isaac and Eliza, was described by the *Baltimore Sun* as a "lawyer, poet, author, lecturer and a minister of the Methodist Episcopal Church, a [R]epublican in politics and a gentleman of wide observation." (See Exhibit 14.) He was also a teacher, published a newspaper, advocated for strict temperance laws, and frequently wrote letters to the editor.

Born in My Lady's Manor, William moved to Baltimore by the early 1860s. He married Fredericka Royston, who came from a prominent family in Baltimore County in the 10th district. The Royston family can be traced back to John Royston, who emigrated in 1727 and died in Baltimore in 1740. Much of the family is buried in the Royston Family Cemetery, now located on the edge of a golf course in Phoenix, Baltimore. Wesley Royston Sr., Fredericka's father, married Mary Fuller, whose father, William Fuller, had been killed during a slave uprising.

William and Fredericka had two sons: Albert Spencer, born Sept. 9, 1869, and Howard Ernest, born Jan. 3, 1877. In 1870, the census lists William's occupation as a teacher. His obituary notes that he taught at the Scheib School in Baltimore, among other places. His brother John was also a teacher there. The Scheib School had been founded by the German Lutheran community in Baltimore, and held classes in both German and English.

In 1872, William Curtis became a minister in the Methodist Episcopal Church. The Methodist Episcopal Church was the first Methodist denomination in the United States, which later became the Methodist Church in 1939 and the present United Methodist Church in 1968.

Surprising a Pastor.—The members and friends of the M. E. Church on Long Green, Baltmore county, surprised their pastor, the Rev. W. C. Griffith. on the evening of the 21st inst., by a visit to the parsonage with some very substantial tokens of their esteem and good will. Turkeys, chickens, hams, beef, a barrel of flour, groceries, horse feed, fuel, and clothing were among' the many good things with which the pastor was remembered.

Baltimore Sun, *Dec. 25, 1877, p. 1.*

In 1880, William Curtis and his family were in Martinsburg, West Virginia, where William Curtis was a preacher and also founded the *Blue Ridge Chronicles*, a weekly newspaper that had a "brief existence," according to his obituary.

He moved with his family to Hagerstown, Maryland, before 1890, where he would remain the rest of his life. He had a law office there and is frequently mentioned in the newspapers as having performed marriages at the office. His law practice included litigation against saloon owners, which sought to close or limit alcohol sales. He published several books:

Chosen Vessels (Baltimore: 1883)

Twice Born: or, Life of Bartholomew Barthol (Baltimore: King, 1886)

Gifts Without Graces, or, Life at Powhatan (Hagerstown, Md.: Morning News, 1895)

The Beebees of Virginia (Hagerstown, Md.: Hagerstown Electric Printery, 1906).

Rev. W. C. Griffith.

Drawing of William Curtis Griffith that appeared in his books.

"Chosen Vessels," by R. W. C. Griffith, of the Baltimore Conference M. E. Church. Baltimore: D. H. Carroll. — "Chosen Vessels" is designed to teach truth under the guise of a romance. The scenes are many of them laid in Maryland, and the writer has obviously an excellent knowledge of "My Lady's Manor" and other portions of the State. The ending tells us by what different paths diverse persons and contrasted natures are led to the same end at last, and to obey the same call to work for the advancement of religion. The studies are manifestly from life, and their surroundings such as Mr. Griffith must have been familiar with in his itineracy as a Methodist minister—both of which facts give a realistic air to the narrative.

Baltimore Sun, *April 24, 1883, p. 5.*

Fredericka Royston died on January 20, 1893 and was buried at the Jessops United Methodist Church in Sparks, Maryland, one of the churches where William Curtis was a circuit preacher. As a circuit preacher, William Curtis was not assigned to one church, but traveled among several churches—including several like the one at Jessops in My Lady's Manor—as a preacher.

William Curtis married Julia Belle Harbaugh on May 28, 1896 in Hagerstown, and they had one daughter, Ruth E., on January 12, 1897. After William died, Julia married George Brewer, but did not have any more children. She died on March 26, 1931. Ruth lived in Washington, D.C., her entire life, working in government service. According to the census, her occupations included clerk in the War Department (1920), statistician (1930), and clerk for the Department of Agriculture (1940). Ruth never married, and died on March 21, 1971. Ruth and her mother are buried in a traditional German-American cemetery, Prospect Hills, in Washington, D.C.

William Curtis died on April 27, 1913 and is buried with Fredericka, at the cemetery at the United Methodist Church in Jessops, Maryland. (See Exhibit 15 for William's obituary.)

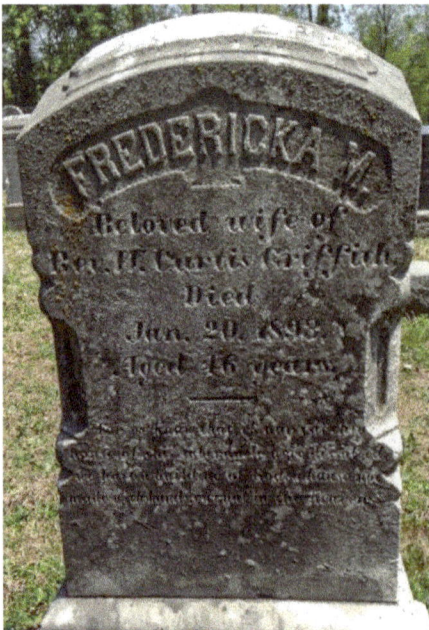

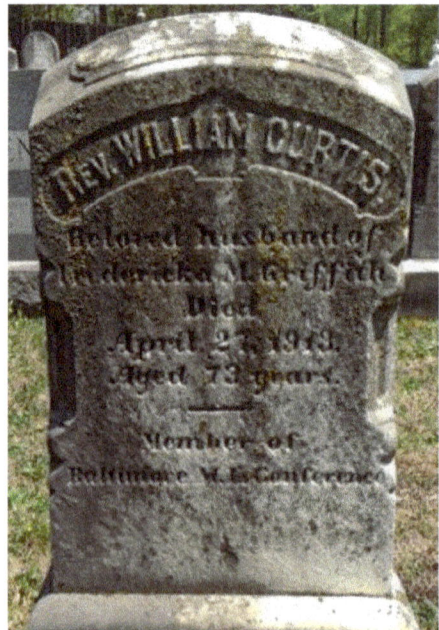

Albert Spencer Griffith
September 9, 1869–August 23, 1928

Albert Spencer Griffith was also a teacher, living most of his life in Camden and Burlington, New Jersey. He was a principal for a public school in Camden and later a superintendent of schools in Burlington.

He married Almira Taylor on April 4, 1894, in a ceremony officiated by Rev. W. C. Griffith. Albert and Almira had one son, Raymond Spencer Griffith, who was born on June 9, 1895. Almira died on January 8, 1898, and she is buried in her family's plot in Louden Cemetery, Baltimore.

Albert later married Evelyn Clark on June 21, 1899. They had no children.

Raymond Spencer Griffith served in World War I and later was a banker. He died on January 1, 1966. He was married to Anne Millett Whitehead; they had one son, Donald Spencer Griffith, who was born in June 1921. Anne died on December 13, 1988.

Donald Spencer Griffith died on December 9, 1994. He was married to Alta Hansen, who died on September 27, 2006. They had four children: Norma Lee, William, Gail (Crawford), and Robert Spencer. Robert Spencer died in 1976.

Albert Spencer and Evelyn are buried at Odd Fellows Cemetery in Camden, New Jersey. Raymond Spencer Griffith is buried in West Laurel Hill Cemetery in Bala Cynwyd, Pennsylvania. Anne (Whitehead) Griffith, Donald Spencer Griffith, and Alta (Hansen) Griffith and Donald and Alta's son Robert are buried at Hillside Cemetery, Roslyn, Pennsylvania.

Howard Ernest Griffith
January 3, 1877–March 29, 1950

Howard Ernest Griffith.

Howard married Florence Hitch Phillips (1861–1921) in 1907 and lived in Baltimore. Florence had been married to Charles Norris, who had died in 1893. Florence had received an inheritance from her mother, after contesting her mother's will. The 1910 census lists them as living at 1601 N. Monroe, Baltimore, with Howard working as a salesman for "Naval Stores."

On February 15, 1915, Charles Ernest Griffith was born, the son of Nellie Phillips and Howard Griffith. Nellie was Florence's niece. Nellie, born in Princess Anne, Maryland, was living with her aunt and uncle in order to finish school. The baby, however, was raised as the child of Howard and Florence, and, by all accounts, Howard and Florence became estranged from the Phillips family.

In 1920, Howard, Florence, and Charles lived in Washington, D.C., at the Portner Apartments. Howard lists "none" as his occupation on the 1920 census form. There is also a nurse listed as living with the family. Later that year they moved to Philadelphia, where Florence could receive treatment for a cardiac problem. She died there on May 14, 1921; she was buried in Louden Park Cemetery with her first husband, Charles Norris, in a plot very close to those of her parents.

On November 25, 1922, Howard married Teresa Mae Riddlemoser (born July 23, 1875), who came from a wealthy family from Baltimore. They lived the rest of their lives in New York City.

The 1925 New York State Census lists the family as living at 296 Central Park West, with Howard listed as "retired." The census raises a mystery: in addition to Charles, a daughter, Tessie, 8 years old, is listed. No further information about "Tessie" can be found; she does not appear, for example, in the 1930 census (although she would have been just 13 years old) or in any of the later census documents or other documents. She may have been the daughter of Teresa from her prior marriage, and, perhaps, died as a young girl.

The 1930 census lists Howard, Teresa, and Charles as living on Riverside Drive. Howard is listed as a salesman for "chemicals," and Charles is in school. By 1940, Howard and Teresa are living on West 88th Street, and, in 1950, are living at 51 W. 89th Street.

Howard Ernest Griffith died on March 29, 1950, in the City Hospital; he was cremated. His death certificate lists his occupation as "general salesman, industrial alcohol." Teresa died in New York on December 6, 1954.

Charles Ernest Griffith
February 15, 1915–February 24, 2005

Charles Ernest Griffith.

Charles Ernest—Grandpa—was born on February 15, 1915 in Baltimore and moved to New York City with his father, Howard, after 1921.

On September 16, 1936, in New York City, Charles married Amalie Louise Guenther.

Family Tree

William Henry Phillips 1816–1886 — married — **Annie Hitch Lankford** 1835–1909

Children:
- **Samuel Oscar Phillips** 1856–
- **William James Phillips** 1857–1921
- **Florence Amanda Pollitt** 1862–1951
- **Lalah Anne Phillips** 1859–1939
- **Florence Hitch Phillips** 1861–1921

Children of William James Phillips and Florence Amanda Pollitt:
- **Clarence Wilson Phillips** 1887–1985
- **Ada Anne Phillips** 1892–1982
- **Anne Hitch Phillips** 1900–1984
- **James Weldon Phillips** 1905–1972
- **William Roger Phillips** 1889–1974
- **Margaret A. Phillips** 1896–1947
- **Nellie Frances Phillips** 1895–1920

Nellie Frances Phillips 1895–1920 — married — **Howard Ernest Griffith** 1877–1950

Child:
- **Charles Ernest Griffith** 1915–2005

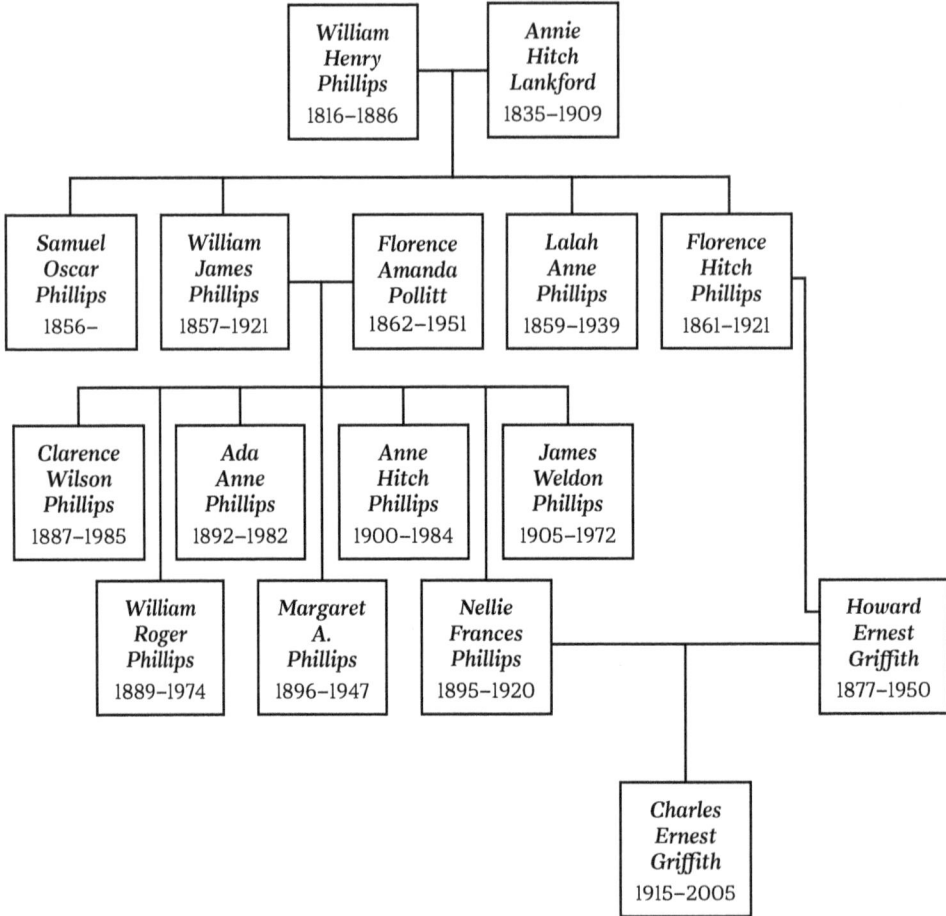

Descendants of William Henry Phillips and Annie Hitch Lankford

Phillips

William Henry Phillips
1816–July 26, 1886

Captain William Henry Phillips lived in Baltimore and was a mariner on the Chesapeake River. He married Annie Hitch Lankford, who was from a very old Somerset County family that traces back to Thomas Lankford, born in England in 1620. Lankford's son John Lankford immigrated to Somerset County in 1676; his descendant Benjamin Lankford (1765–1812) married Nancy Hitch (1775–1822). The Hitch family name would be passed down to their granddaughter Annie Hitch Lankford, who in turn would pass it down to her daughter Florence Hitch Phillips, and to another granddaughter.

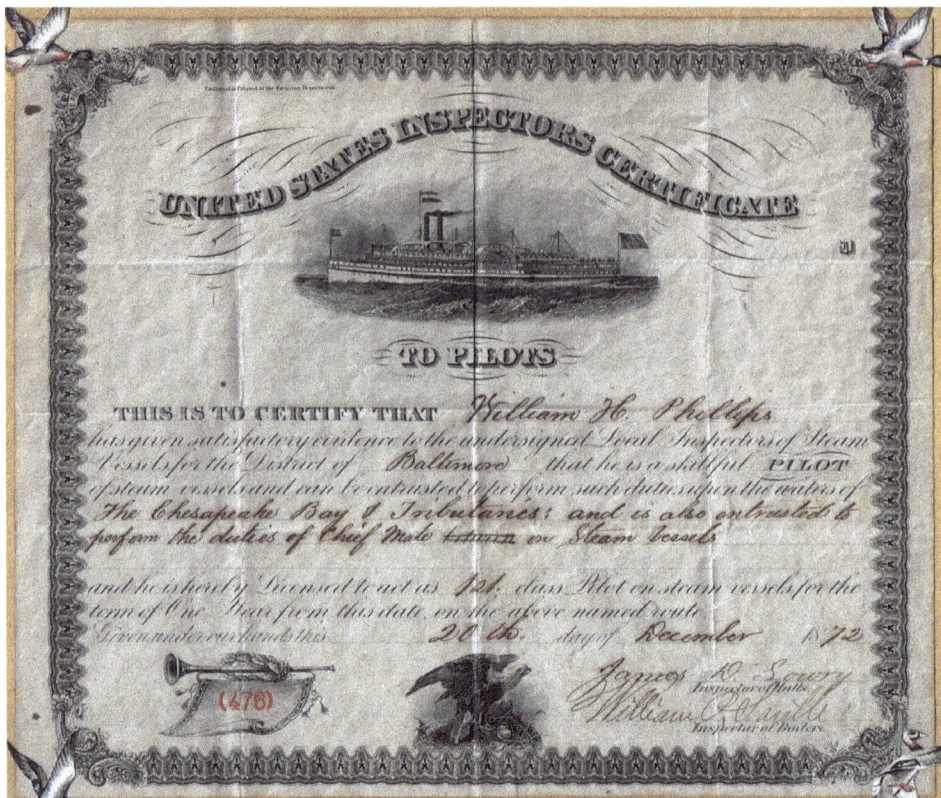

*William Henry Phillips's license to be a steam vessel pilot
and chief mate in Chesapeake Bay.*

*William Henry Phillips with sons
William James, at left, and
Samuel Oscar, at right.*

William and Annie had four children: Samuel Oscar (b. 1856); William James (b. 1857); Lalah Anne (b. 1859); and Florence Hitch (b. 1861).

Their son Samuel Oscar also became a mariner. Although not confirmed, the Phillips descendants report that they were always told that Samuel was responsible for the sinking of the steamship *Oceanic*, while it was hauling stone on the Chesapeake Bay. The financial loss was significant, and Samuel Oscar moved "west."

William James Phillips is Nellie's father, and is discussed below.

Lalah Anne married James Francis Covington and had three children. She died April 7, 1939.

Florence married Howard Ernest Griffith.

William Henry died from Bright's disease on July 26, 1886. Annie Hitch Lankford died March 26, 1909. They are buried in Louden Park Cemetery, Section YY, in Baltimore County. Their daughter Lalah Anne is buried in the same plot, and their daughter Florence Hitch (Phillips) (Norris) Griffith is buried nearby.

When Annie died, she was living with her daughter Lalah, and left Lalah much of her estate, which was valued at $8,000 in 1909 dollars. Florence Griffith had been left an income of $500 for life, and she challenged the will. The dispute was apparently settled out of court.

William James Phillips
November 29, 1857–March 11, 1921

William James Phillips.

William James Phillips was a farmer, operated a general store, was sheriff of Somerset County, and owned a substantial amount of property in and around Princess Anne. On November 10, 1886, he married Florence Amanda Pollitt in Somerset County, and moved from Baltimore to Princess Anne.

Florence Amanda Pollitt (July 26, 1862–August 14, 1951) was from two very old Somerset County families— on her father's side, the Pollitts; on her mother's side, the Haymans.

Notes from the Phillips General Store.

William James and Florence Amanda had seven children:

1. Clarence Wilson Phillips (Nov. 1, 1887–March 24, 1985), who lived in Princess Anne his entire life, married Florence Bounds (July 29, 1885–1970). They had two children, Clarence Wilson Phillips Jr. (Oct. 30, 1916–Oct. 10, 2003) and George Lee Phillips (July 9, 1922–April 19, 1995). George, who lost a leg during World War I, later married and had five children. He

is buried in Arlington National Cemetery. Clarence Wilson Phillips Jr. was a teacher; he married Amy Adelle "Mamie" Lagates (Sept. 23, 1923–June 28, 2010). Late in life, Charles Griffith (Grandpa) met Clarence Wilson Phillips (they were first cousins)— the only Phillips relative Grandpa ever met.

2. William Roger Phillips (Nov. 16, 1889–March 2, 1974) lived in Chester, Pennsylvania, and married Mary Dickson.

3. Ada Anne Phillips (Oct. 29, 1892–April 28, 1982) married John H. Jett (July 13, 1888–Dec. 1976). She was a teacher; she never had any children.

4. Nellie Frances Phillips (Nov. 11, 1895–Feb. 8, 1920).

5. Margaret A. Phillips (Feb. 1896–March 23, 1947) married Paul B. Brown; they had two sons, Paul L. Brown and Jerry P. Brown.

6. Anne Hitch Phillips (Nov. 11, 1900–Nov. 7, 1984) married Albert W. Van Zandt (Dec. 8, 1900–Jan. 27, 1974). They had two children: W. Robert Van Zandt and James Cameron Van Zandt.

7. James Weldon Phillips Sr. (July 17, 1905–Nov. 9, 1972) married Mary Verna Perkins (May 14, 1910–2006); he worked as an electrical engineer and lived in Prospect Park, Pennsylvania. They had three children: James Weldon Phillips Jr. (b. Aug. 21, 1938), Susan V. Phillips (b. and d. 1944), and Marilyn Phillips (b. May 25, 1949).

In 1912, the Phillipses were involved in an incident that was widely covered in the newspapers. Their daughter Maggie (Margaret), who was then 16 years old, was assaulted; the assailant later threatened Maggie and her mother if they reported the crime. The assailant was almost lynched, and the local sheriff was forced to flee with his prisoner in order to protect him. (See Exhibit 16.) After a trial, the assailant was hanged in Princess Anne.

A few years later, William James and Florence Amanda's second child, William Roger (who was always called Roger), was working as a sheriff's deputy in Somerset County and was involved in an incident that resulted in another man being shot to death. Roger was repeatedly physically threatened, and the family felt it necessary to leave Somerset County. As a result, William James and Florence Amanda and their children Roger, Ada, Maggie, Anne, and James relocated to Upland, Delaware, and later to Chester, Pennsylvania.

Clarence remained in Somerset County, and Nellie left to study in Baltimore.

William James returned to Princess Anne, and died there on March 11, 1921. Florence Amanda died in August, 1951; she is buried with her husband in the Manokin Presbyterian Cemetery in Princess Anne, Maryland. Sadly, neither of their obituaries mention their daughter Nellie or their grandson Charles Ernest Griffith, or in the case of Florence, the Griffith great-grandchildren. (See Exhibits 17 and 18). Clarence Sr. and his wife, Florence, Ada and John Jett, and Nellie are also buried in the family plot.

Nellie Frances Phillips
November 11, 1895–February 8, 1920

Nellie Frances Phillips.

After her son was born, Nellie remained in Baltimore, where she worked as a secretary for an insurance company. She died from bronchial pneumonia at the age of 24 and was buried in the family plot in Princess Anne. Her obituary (Exhibit 19) tragically makes no mention of her son.

During the research for this book, I was able to make contact with James Van Zandt, a son of Anne Hitch Phillips, as well as other relatives. James and Charles Ernest (Grandpa) were first cousins, although they never knew each other. The Phillips descendants had always wondered what had become of Nellie's son, and were as delighted as I was to learn the rest of the story.

Nellie with a dog.

Nellie's locket had been kept in the family for all these years, and was sent to me.

Charles Ernest Griffith
& Amalie Louise Guenther

Amalie Louise Guenther.

Charles Ernest Griffith.

CHARLES ERNEST GRIFFITH and Amalie Louise Guenther were married on September 16, 1936.

By the time of the 1940 census, Grandpa was living with Gammy and their new son, Charles Ernest ("Chuck") Griffith Jr., born on September 12, 1937 in Hempstead, New York.

Alan Richard Griffith would be born December 1941, and David Edward Griffith would be born on October 26, 1953.

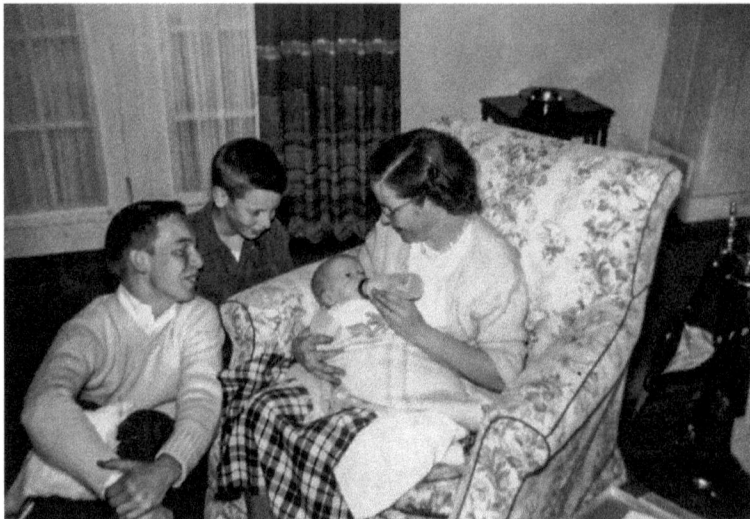

Amalie with Chuck, Alan, and Dave.

The family moved to Pound Ridge, to the house on Trinity Pass. After Grandpa's retirement, they moved to Dorset, Vermont, and St. John's Island, Florida. Toward the ends of their lives, they moved from Vermont to Centerville, Maryland.

POUND RIDGE

Rambling Country Home

On 5 beautiful acres bordered on 2 sides by forests & a river. It's in the choicest area of Pound Ridge. Some of the house dates back to the 1800's with beams & hand woodwork. Entry hall, living room w/fireplace & French doors leading to the lovely gardens. Den w/old beams, bath, eat-in kitchen & sun room w/door leading to landscaped in-ground pool w/cabana. Upstairs a marvelous Master bedroomw/fireplace...3 more bedrooms & bath. The detached garage also has a studio w/cathedral ceiling & stone fireplace. Beautiful gardens & rock outcroppings make this one of Pound Ridge's most appealing settings. $149,500

EXCLUSIVE AGENT

HOULIHAN

Scotts Corners, Pound Ridge 764-5762
Depot Plaza, Katonah   232-5007

The house in Pound Ridge and the listing for when it was purchased.

Amalie Louise Guenther Griffith died in Centerville, Maryland on February 27, 2000. She is buried at the Old Wye Church; Charles Ernest Griffith, who died in Vero Beach, Florida, on February 24, 2005, is buried with her.

Exhibits

Exhibit 1

Newspaper article from the Piney Point Archives

Vereins-Zeitung des Turnverein Gera-R.

Nr. 9   Mai 1932   9. Jahrg.

Nachruf.

Es starben: im 75. Lebensjahr am 1. Osterfeiertag infolge Herzschlag unser Vereinigungsmitglied ehem. Brückenturner **Otto Koch;**

im 74. Lebensjahr Donnerst., den 7. April unser Vereinigungsmitglied ehem. Brückenturner **Paul Lecker;**

im 71. Lebensjahr Sonntag, den 24. April unser Vereinigungsmitglied ehem. Brückenturner **Richard Freund.**

Wir verlieren in ihnen drei treue Anhänger unserer Vereinigung und der Turnverein Gera drei ehemalige tüchtige Turner bezw. Vorturner. Richard Freund war in den 80 er Jahren einer der besten Vorturner unseres Vereins und bis vor kurzem noch als turnendes Mitglied der Männerriege 1888 tätig. — Ihr Andenken werden wir in Ehren halten!

Leitung der ehem. Bellevue- und Brückenturner, i. A.: Paul Munnecke.

Nachruf.

Es starben die Turnbrüder

Otto Koch - Paul Lecker - Richard Freund - Gustav Fuchs.

Wir wissen, daß sie uns alle liebe, treue Turnbrüder waren. Vergessen werden wir sie nie! Ihr Andenken ist uns heilig!   Der Turnrat.

August Günther

Vereins-Ehrenvorsitzender, geb. d. 28. 1. 1832, gest. d. 6. 7. 1908.

Ehret die Alten!

Das Bild August Günthers, welches unser großes Vereinszimmer ziert, ruft manche Erinnerung an längst vergangene Zeiten wach.

Ich will versuchen, den turnerischen Lebenslauf dieses alten treuen Turnbruders in kurzen Zügen den Turnschwestern und Turnbrüdern vor Augen zu führen.

August Günther trat am 23. April 1851 als 19 jähriger Zeugmachergeselle unserem Verein bei und wurde laut Vereinsbeschluß mit zu den Vereinsgründern gezählt. Als Freund des Gesangs beteiligte er sich mit an der Bildung einer Gesangsabteilung, deren Gründungstag der 4. Juni 1851 war. Als am 22. September 1851 das erste Vereinschauturnen abgehalten wurde, turnte er schon tüchtig mit und brachte es in den nächsten Jahren bis zum Vorturner. Als am 27. August 1859 eine freiwillige Turnerfeuerwehr gegründet wurde, betrauten ihn die Turnbrüder mit einer Zugführerstelle. Beim zweiten großen Vereinschauturnen am 19. August 1860 turnte er einer Riege als Vorturner vor. Auch beim Turnunterricht an Schulkinder in den Jahren 1859 bis 1861 vertrat er Vorturnerdienste. Als Vertreter des Vereins war er bei Gründung des Osterländischen Turngaues im Jahre 1873 mit tätig. Bereits am 28. Januar 1863 zum Ehrenmitglied des Vereins ernannt, war er bis zum 25 jährigen Vereinsjubiläum selbst das älteste Vereinsehrenmitglied. Am 7. März 1877 zog er mit vom Vereinslokal „Bellevue" nach dem neuen Vereinslokal „Heinrichsbrücke" und mußte den großen Rückgang an Vereinsmitgliedern bis Ende 1878 mit erleben. Daß der Verein vom Jahre 1879 die fürstliche Gymnasialturnhalle benutzen durfte, war sein Verdienst. Als im Jahre 1883 der Reußische Turngau gegründet wurde, betraute man ihn mit dem Posten des Gaukassierers,

102   Vereinszeitung des Turnvereins Gera, D. T.

viele Jahre gehörte er dem Gauturnrat an. 1896 mußte er den Abbruch der Gymnasialturnhalle mit erleben, nachdem er als Vertreter des Vereins alles Mögliche getan hatte, dies zu verhindern durch einen eventuellen Ankauf der Turnhalle durch den Verein.

Die Grundsteinlegung der Lützowturnhalle am 16. August 1896 und die Einweihung derselben am 19./20. Juni 1897 waren für ihn schöne Erinnerungstage.

August Günther war von seinem 19. bis zum 77. Lebensjahre Mitglied unseres Vereins und einer von den wenigen, denen es vergönnt war, an der Entwicklung unseres Vereins 57 Jahre tätig teilzunehmen.

Wir wollen in diesem Jahre, in welchem er vor 100 Jahren geboren wurde, seiner ehrend gedenken und ihm für seine Treue über das Grab hinaus danken.   Paul Munnecke.

Unsere Turnbewegung in 1. Vierteljahr 1932.

Die Vorturnerschaft

turnte an 7 besonderen Übungsabenden mit 71 Teilnehmern. Durchschnitt pro Abend 10 Teilnehmer. Bestbesuchter Abend am 13. 1. 32 mit 13 Turnern. Schlechtestbesuchter Abend am 25. 3. 32 mit 8 Turnern. 5 Stunden und mehr besuchten Hermann Weimar, Heinz Baumgärtel je 7, Paul Meißner, Erich Encke je 6, Erich Prell, Hans Küffner je 5 Abende.

Außerdem wurde eine Lehrstunde für Knabenvorturner abgehalten. Hieran beteiligten sich 9 Vorturner.

Die Allgemeine Turnabteilung

bestehend aus jüngeren Turnern und Jugendturnern übte an 23 Abenden mit insgesamt 1412 Teilnehmern. Durchschnittsbesuch pro Abend 61 Turner. Bestbesuchter Abend am 5. 2. 32 mit 72 Turnern. Schlechtestbesuchter Abend am 18. 3. 32 mit 49 Turnern. 26 Turner besuchten 20 und mehr Übungsstunden und zwar je 23 Hermann Weimar, Willi Ackermann, Paul Meißner, Heinz Baumgärtel, Hans Küffner, Paul Scheibe, Karl Rußbild, Kurt Höpfner, Herbert Erler, Horst Neidhardt, Helmut Hofmann. Je 22 Erich Encke, Ernst Brünner, Hugo Partsch, Rudolf Barbora, Herbert Helm, Heinz Lohse, Stephan Dietsch. Je 21 Fritz Rudorf, Heinz Müller, Alfred Fiedler, Herbert Freund. Je 20 Erich Mehlhorn, Herbert Lange, Heinz Lange, Heinz Barbora. Beim Schauturnen am 7. Februar beteiligte sich die Abteilung mit 66 Turnern in 8 Riegen.

Die Männerabteilung (Mittwochsabtlg.)

besteht aus 4 Männerriegen und turnte an 13 Abenden mit 452 Turnern. Durchschnitt pro Abend 34 Teilnehmer. Bestbesuchter Abend 27. 1. 32 mit 42 Turnern, schlechtester Abend am 10. 2. 32 mit 28 Turnern. 11 und mehr Übungsstunden besuchten 22 Turner und zwar je 13 die Turnbrüder: Greil, Kretschmar, Müller, Päz, Theilig, Eger, Gäbler, Renner, Alenstedt, Bachmann, Schwalbe, Lohe, Claus, Zipfel, Willi Ackermann. Je 12 Tbr. Albin Kneisel, Ficker, Franz Schuhmann, Habermann, Weigel. Je 11 Tbr. Läsker und Richard Martin. Beim Schauturnen beteiligte sich die Abteilung mit 33 Turnern in 3 Riegen.

Die Knabenabteilung

besteht zur Zeit aus 2 Abteilungen in 9 Riegen. Die jüngeren unter 10 Jahren turnen in 2 Riegen von nachmittags 5—6 Uhr, die älteren über 10 Jahre an den gleichen Tagen (Dienstag u. Freitag) von 6—7.30 Uhr. An 23 Übungstagen nahmen insgesamt 1832 Knaben teil. In der gleichen Zeit im Vorjahr turnten 1436 Knaben. Also ein Mehr von 396 Teilnehmern. Durchschnitt pro Übungsstunde 80 Knaben. Im Vorjahr 57 Knaben. Rekordhöchstbesuch am 8. 1. 32 mit 94 Teilnehmern. Niedrigster Turnbesuch am 9. 2. 32 mit 59 Teilnehmern. 20 und mehr Übungsstunden besuchten 29 Knaben und zwar je 23 Helmut Bergmann, Heinz Krause I, Gerhard Körbel, Kurt Renner, Helmut Eichler, Heinz Neumeister, Fritz Neumeister, je 22 Stunden Hans Behr, Herbert Bergmann, Rudolf Donnerhack, Hans Meister, Walter Mühlbach, Karl Eisfeld, Siegried Zipfel, Waldemar Meier, je 21 Stunden Heinz Thießen, Hans Bräutigam, Erich Weiß, Hilmar Adolph, Werner Künzel, Wolfgang

Exhibit 2

Translation

SOCIETY NEWSPAPER OF THE GYMNASTICS SOCIETY GERA-R

No. 9   May 1932   9th volume

OBITUARY.

Our society member former Gymnast, **Otto Koch,**
passed away in the 75th year of his life on the 1st Easter holiday as the result of a heart attack;
Our society member former Gymnast, **Paul Lecker,**
passed away in the 74th year of his life, Thursday the 7th of April;
Our society member former Gymnast, **Richard Freund,**
passed away in the 71st year of his life, Sunday the 24th of April.
In them, we are losing three loyal supporters of our society; and the Gymnastics Society Gera
three formerly capable gymnasts, or demonstrators. Richard Freund was one of the best demonstrators of our
society, in the 80s, and was an active as a practicing gymnast in the 1888 men's team, until recently. – We will
continue to honor their memories!

Leadership of the former Bellevue and Brüden-gymnasts, on behalf of Paul Munnende.

OBITUARY

Our gymnast brothers:

OTTO KOCH - PAUL LEDER - RICHARD FREUND - GUSTAV FUCHS

Have passed away.
We know that they all were our beloved, loyal gymnast brothers. We will never forget them!
Their memory is sacred to us!   THE GYMNASTICS COUNCIL.

AUGUST GÜNTHER

HONORARY CHAIRMAN OF THE SOCIETY, BORN ON 28 JAN 1832, DECEASED ON 6 JUL 1908.

HONOR THE ELDERS!

August Günther's picture, which adorns our society's large room, evokes some memories of times long bygone.
I will attempt to create a brief visual of this old, loyal gymnast-brother's gymnast-life for the gymnast-masters and gymnast-brothers.
August Günther joined our gymnastics society as a 19 year old cloth-maker's journeyman on the 23rd of April 1851 and was, by decree of
the society, considered to be one of the founding members of the society. As a friend of singing, he partook in the creation of a singing
department, whose founding date was the 4th of June 1851. When the first society gymnastic display was held on the 22nd of September
1851, he was already practicing gymnastics capably and made it to a demonstrator over the next years.
When a voluntary gymnast's fire department was founded on the 27th of August 1859, the gymnast-brothers entrusted him with the
position of a station officer. During the second great society gymnastic display on the 19th of August 1860, he practices as a demonstrator
for one of the gymnastic squads. Even for gymnastics classes for school children, during the years from 1859 until 1861, he served as a
demonstrator. As a representative of the society, he was involved in the founding of the Osterland gymnast-region (Turngau Osterland),
in the year 1873. Already promoted to an honorary member of the Gymnastic Society on the 28th of January 1863, he was the oldest living
honorary member of the society, until the society's 25th anniversary.
On the 7th of March 1877 he joined the move from the society's premises "Bellevue" to the society's new premises "Heinrichsbrücke" and
had to experience the decline of society members until the end of 1878.
That the society was allowed to use the prince's Grammar-school's gymnasium from the year 1879 onwards, was due to him. When the
Russian gymnast-region (Turngau) was founded in 1883, he was entrusted with the post as the region's cashier.

102   Society Newspaper of the Gymnastics Society Gera, D: F.

he belonged to the regional gymnastics council for many years. He had to witness the destruction of the grammar school's Gymnasium, after he had done everything possible to prevent this via a potential purchase of the gymnasium by the society, as a representative of the society. The groundbreaking of the Lükow-Gymnasium on the 16th of August 1896 and its inauguration on the 19/20 of June 1897 were days of fond memories for him.

August Günther was a member of our society from his 19th until his 77th year of age, and was one of the few, who were fortunate enough to partake in the development of our society for 57 years.

In this year, in which he was born 100 years ago, we want to commemorate him in honor and want to thank him for his loyalty beyond the grave.   Paul Munnede.

Our gymnastics movements in the 1st quarter, 1932.

The demonstrators

practiced gymnastics on 7 special training evenings with 71 participants. Average per evening 10 participants. Evening with most visitors 13 JAN 32 with 13 gymnasts. Evening with the worst number of visitors was on 25 MAR 32 with 8 gymnasts. 5 sessions and more were visited by Hermann Wiemar, Heinz Baumgärter each visited 7, Paul Meißner, Erich Ende each 5, Erich Press, Hans Hüffner each 5 evenings. Additionally a training session for boy demonstrators was conducted, 9 demonstrators partook in this.

The general gymnastics department

consisting of younger gymnasts and young-gymnasts, trained on 23 evenings with altogether 1412 participants. Average per evening 61 gymnasts. The most visited evening was 18 MAR 32 with 49 gymnasts. 26 gymnasts visited 20 or more evening lessons and 23 each Hermann Weimar, Willi Adermann, Paul Meißner, Heinz Baumgärtel, Hans Küffner, Paul Scheibe, Karl Rußbile, Karl Höpfner, Herbert Erler, Horst Reidhardt, Helmust Hofmann. 22 each Erich Ende, Ernst Brünner, Hugo Bartsch, Rudolf Barbara, Herbert Helm, Heinz Lohse, Stepan Dietrsch. 21 each Fritz Rudorf, Heinz Müller, Alfred Fiedler, Herbert Freund. 20 each Erich Mehlhorn, Herbert Lange, Heinz Lange, Heinz Barbara. During the gymnastics display on the 7th of February, the department partook with 66 gymnasts in 8 squads.

The men's department (Wednesday department)

consists of 4 male squads and exercised on 13 evenings with 452 gymnasts. Average per evening, 34 participants. Most visited evening 27 JAN 32 with 42 gymnasts. Least visited evening on 10 FEB 32 with 28 gymnasts. 11 and more evening lessons were visited by 22 gymnasts and 13 each the gymnast-brothers: Greil, Kretschmar, Müller, Pätz, Theilig, Eger, Gäbler, Renner, Alenstedt, Bachmann, Schwalbe, Loße, Claus, Zipfel, Willi Adermann. 12 each Ibr. Ulbin Knfeifel, Fider, Franz Schuhmann, Habermann, Weigel. 11 each Ibr. Läster and Richard Martin. During the gymnastics display the department partook with 33 gymnasts in 3 squads.

The boy's department

currently consists out of 2 departments in 9 squads. The younger boys under the age of 10 exercise in squads, in the afternoons 5-6PM, the older ones over the age of 10 practice on the same days (Tuesday and Friday) from 6.p-7.30p. On 23 practicing days, a total of 1832 boys partook. At the same time, in the previous year, 1436 boys exercised gymnastics. Therefore, an increase of 396 participants. Average per lesson was 80 boys. 57 boys in the previous year. Highest recorded visit on 8 JAN 32 with 94 participants. Lowest number of visits on 9 FEB 32 with 59 participants. 20 and more lessons were visited by 29 boys and 23 each by Helmut Bergmann, Heinz Krause 1, Gerhard Körbel, Kurt Renner, Helmut Eichler, Heinz Neumeister, Fritz Neumeister. 22 hours each Hans Behr, Herbert Bergmann, Rudolf Donnerhaf, Hans Meister, Walter Mühlbach, Karl Eisfeld, Siegried Zipfel, Waldemar Meier; 21 hours each Heinz Thießen, Hans Bräutigam, Erich Weiß, Hilmer Adolph, Werner Künzel, Wolfgang

Exhibit 3

Guenther Christmas Card List
Piney Point Archives

CHRISTMAS GREETINGS   1932

o	Allen, Dr. & Mrs. J. Wilford	117 West 12th Street, New York, N.Y.
	Amalie, Aunt - Mother Cecilie, Urseline Convent, Armidale, New South Wales, Australia.	
	Arnheim, Mr. & Mrs. Albert A.	336 Nuber Avenue, Mount Vernon, N.Y.
o	Beveridge, Mr. & Mrs. Murray J.	39 Rockridge Road, Mount Vernon, N.Y.
o	Brown, Rev. Melford Losee,	133 Glenn Avenue, Mount Vernon, N.Y.
	Clark, Mr. Joshua A.	200 West 54th Street, New York, N.Y.
	Coates, Mr. & Mrs. Ernest	197 Cottage Street, Pawtucket, R.I.
	Coward, Mrs. Harry E. and family	27 Philadelphia Avenue, West Pittston, Pa.
	Decknatel, Mr. & Mrs. F.H.	234 Summit Avenue, Mount Vernon, N.Y.
	Deike, Mr. & Mrs. Wm. F.	152 Cottage Avenue, Mount Vernon, N.Y.
	Dietrich, Paul	18 Poststrasse, St. Gall, Switzerland
o	Durschang, Dr. & Mrs. Anthony C.	425 Riverside Drive, New York, N.Y.
	Eisinger, Mr. & Mrs. L.W.	209 East Sidney Avenue, Mount Vernon, N.Y.
	Everhart, Rev. & Mrs. Rollind O.	Eastern Avenue, Ossining, N.Y.
	Fee, Mr. & Mrs. Wilfred L.	58 North Columbus Avenue, Mount Vernon, NY
	Friedrichs, Mr. & Mrs. Arthur C.	380 Riverside Drive, New York, N.Y.
	Geiger, Mr. and Mrs. Karl	323 Fingerboard Road, St. George, Staten Island
o	Geisler, Dr. & Mrs. Joseph F.	1014 Trinity Avenue, New York, N.Y.
	Gerken, Mrs. Marie - c/o Mr. Adolph Ast, 48 Tuxedo Road, Montclair, N.J.	
	Gerlach, Mr. & Mrs. Philip	38 Forster Avenue, Mount Vernon, N.Y.
	Giraud, Chas. F. Mr. & Mrs.	4293 Vireo Avenue (corner 235th Street) New York, N.Y.
	Guenther, Mr. & Mrs. Alfred	Schmelzhuetten Strasse #14, Gera, Reuss, GERMANY
	Guenther, Mr. & Mrs. August	Schulstrasse #18, Gera, Reuss, GERMANY
	Guenther, Mr. & Mrs. Walter	Stadtbad, Poessneck 1/T, GERMANY
	Hampson, Mr. & Mrs. Fredk	c/o Mount Tom Silk Co. Inc, Holyoke, Mass.
	Hampson, Mr. & Mrs. Joseph	88 Byers Street, Springfield, Mass.
	Hampson, Mr. & Mrs. Walter	197 Cottage Street, Pawtucket, R.I.
	Hayward, Mr. & Mrs. Harry F.	30 Halstead Place, Rye, N.Y.
	Hein, Mr. & Mrs. Henry E.	40 Sickles Avenue, New York, N.Y.

Scheibe, Paul   Hospitalstrasse #25, Zeitz, Prov. Sachsen,
                                                        GERMANY

Schielinger, Mr. & Mrs. Adolph C.   2 Park Lane, Mount Vernon,   N.Y.

(Schloemer, Mrs. Emilie D.)   425 Riverside Drive, New York, N.Y.

Schmitz, Carl   c/o Frau Anna Kayser, 22 Paul Ehrlichstrasse,
                                       Frankfort am Main,   GERMANY

Schulz, Mr. & Mrs. Carl   309 West 86th Street, New York, N.Y.

Schulenburg, Wolfgang   Waldstrasse #120, Gera, Reuss, GERMANY

Sloat, Mr. & Mrs. J. Wilfred   310 East Sidney Avenue, Mount Vernon, N.Y.

Stromeyer, Mrs. Chas. F. and family   303 Sheridan Blvd, Mount Vernon, N.Y.

~~Stromeyer, Mrs. W.A. and family~~   1008 Trinity Avenue, Bronx, New York

Taylor, Mr. & Mrs. Theodore A. Jr.   195 Fisher Avenue, White Plains, N.Y.

Tischendorf, Selmar Herrn   Talsatrasse #40 III, Gera, Reuss, GERMANY

Vogt, Mr. & Mrs. Adolph W.   111 South Fullerton Avenue, Montclair, N.J.

Vogt, Mrs. George   834 Hermitage Avenue, Chicago, Ill.

~~Williams, Mr. & Mrs. David~~   303 Sheridan Blvd, Sheridan Gardens, Mount
                                                        Vernon, NY

Wilson, Dr. Fredk H.   54 North 21st Street, East Orange, N.J.

Wolfrum, Carl Herman   Aussig a/Elbe, Csechoslovakia

Wuertz, Mrs. OTTO W.   1136 Fifth Avenue, New York, N.Y.

Young, Mr. & Mrs. R.D.   ~~Charle,   (New Brunswikk)~~ CANADA
                              Cedar Springs Ontario

Exhibit 4

Russia *Passenger List*

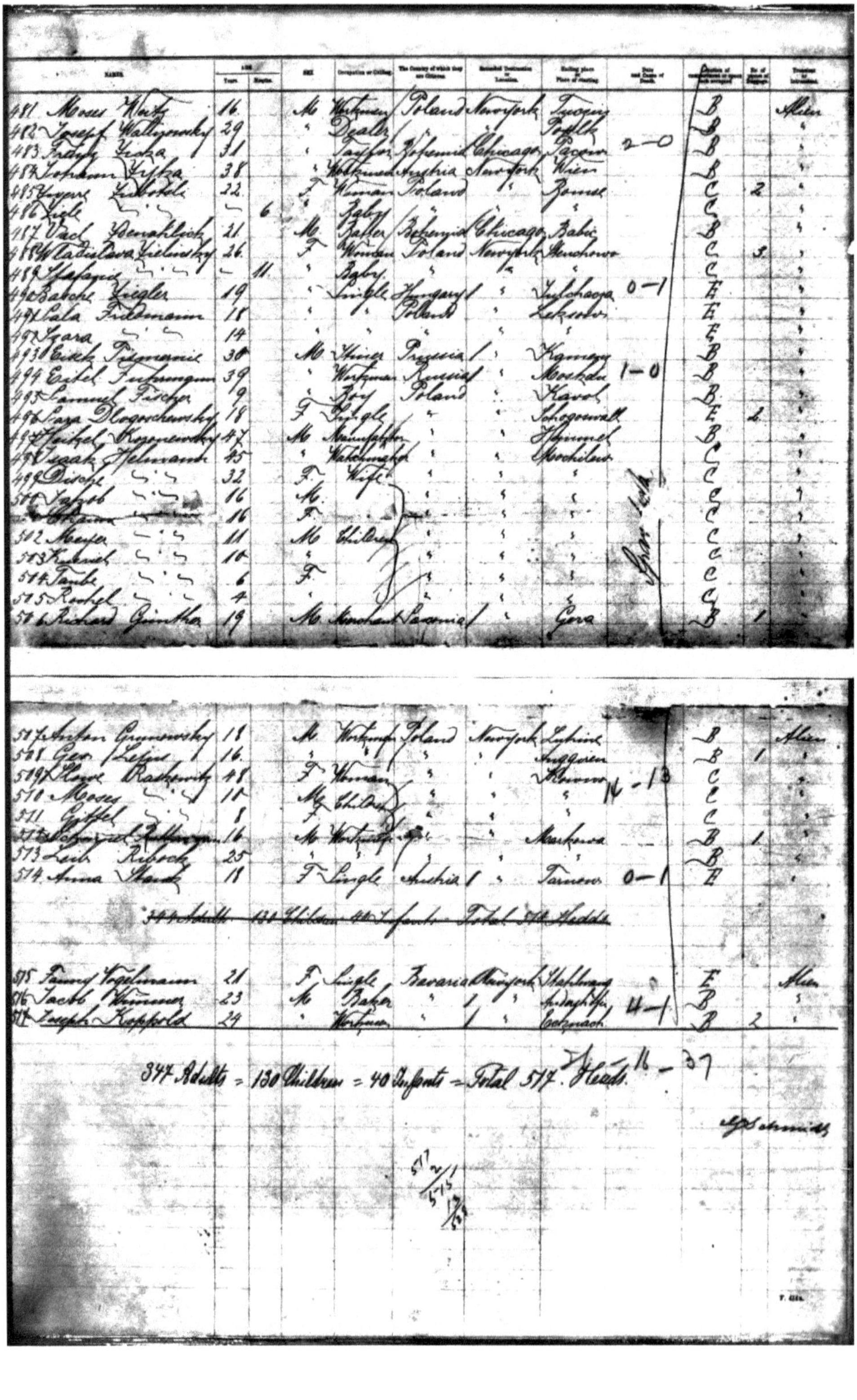

No.	Names	Age: Years	Age: Months	Sex	Occupation or Calling	The Country of which they are Citizens	Intended Destination or Location	Native place or Place of Residence	Date and Cause of Death	Location of compartment	No. of pieces of Baggage	Transient or Intransient
481	Moses [illegible]	16		M	Workman	Poland	New York	[illegible]		B		Alien
482	Josef [illegible]	29		"	Dealer	"	"	[illegible]		B		"
483	[illegible]	31		"	Taylor	Bohemia	Chicago	[illegible]	2—0	B		"
484	Johann [illegible]	38		"	Workman	Austria	New York	Wien		B		"
485	[illegible]	22		F	Woman	Poland	"	[illegible]		C	2	"
486	[illegible] " "	—	6	"	Baby	"	"	"		C		"
487	Vacl [illegible]	21		M	Baker	Bohemia	Chicago	[illegible]		B		"
488	Wladislava [illegible]	26		F	Woman	Poland	New York	[illegible]		C	3	"
489	[illegible] " "	—	11	"	Baby	"	"	"		C		"
490	[illegible] Ziegler	19		"	Single	Hungary	"	[illegible]	0—1	E		"
491	[illegible] Friedmann	18		"	"	Poland	"	[illegible]		E		"
492	[illegible] " "	14		"	"	"	"	"		E		"
493	[illegible]	30		M	[illegible]	Prussia	"	[illegible]		B		"
494	[illegible]	39		"	Workman	Russia	"	[illegible]	1—0	B		"
495	Samuel Fischer	9		"	Boy	Poland	"	[illegible]		B		"
496	[illegible]	18		F	Single	"	"	[illegible]		E	2	"
497	[illegible]	47		M	[illegible]	"	"	[illegible]		B		"
498	[illegible]	45		"	Watchmaker	"	"	[illegible]		C		"
499	[illegible] " "	32		F	Wife	"	"	"		C		"
500	Jakob " "	16		M		"	"	"		C		"
~~[illegible]~~		16		F		"	"	"		C		"
502	Meyer " "	11		M	Children	"	"	"		C		"
503	[illegible] " "	10		"		"	"	"		C		"
504	[illegible] " "	6		F		"	"	"		C		"
505	[illegible] " "	4		"		"	"	"		C		"
506	Richard [illegible]	19		M	Merchant	[illegible]	"	Gora		B	1	"
507	Anton [illegible]	18		M	Workman	Poland	New York	[illegible]		B		Alien
508	[illegible]	16		"	"	"	"	[illegible]		B	1	"
509	[illegible]	48		F	Woman	"	"	[illegible]	14-13	C		"
510	Moses " "	10		M	Children	"	"	"		C		"
511	[illegible] " "	8		F		"	"	"		C		"
~~512~~	~~[illegible]~~	16		M	Workman	"	"	[illegible]		B	1	"
513	[illegible]	25		"	"	"	"	"		B		"
514	Anna [illegible]	18		F	Single	Austria	"	[illegible]	0—1	E		"
	~~344 Adults 130 Children 40 Infants Total 514 Heads~~											
515	[illegible]	21		F	Single	Bavaria	New York	[illegible]		E		Alien
516	Jacob [illegible]	23		M	Baker	"	"	[illegible]	4—1	B		"
517	Joseph [illegible]	24		"	Workman	"	"	[illegible]		B	2	"

347 Adults = 130 Children = 40 Infants = Total 517 Heads. 16 - 37

[illegible signature]

Exhibit 5

Guenther Naturalization Certificate

	8536

Family Name	Given Name or Names
GUNTHER	RICHARD R. S.

Title and Location of Court

U. S. DISTRICT COURT, NEW YORK, N.Y.

Date of Naturalization	Volume or Bundle No.	Page No.	Copy of Record No.
FEB. 24 1899	75	—	448

Address of Naturalized Person

960 E. 169 ST. N.Y.C.

Occupation	Birth Date or Age	Former Nationality
CLERK	AUG 9 1872	GERMAN

Port of Arrival in the United States	Date of Arrival
N. Y. N. Y.	SEPT 10 1891

Names, Addresses and Occupations of Witnesses To Naturalization

1 CHRISTIAN L. SACK 216 W. 112 ST. N.Y.C.
2   MERCHANT

Exhibit 6

Passport Application

37,976

Form for Naturalized Citizen. No. 179.

Printed and sold by Ure & Company, 66 Broadway, N. Y. City.

No. _____ Issued _____

United States of America.

STATE OF *New York*

COUNTY OF *New York* } ss:

I, *Richard R. J. Guenther* A NATURALIZED AND LOYAL CITIZEN OF THE UNITED STATES, do hereby apply to the Department of State at Washington for a passport for *myself and wife* born at *New York City* on the *15th* day of *May* 1 **8**3, and

I do solemnly swear that I was born at *Gera* in *Germany* on or about the *9th* day of *August* 1872; that I emigrated to the United States, sailing on board the *The Prussia* from *Hamburg* on or about the ____ day of *Sept* 1 1891; that I resided *19* years, uninterruptedly, in the United States, from *1891* to *1910* at *New York* that I was naturalized as a citizen of the United States before the *District* Court of *Southern District* at *New York* on the *24th* day of *February* 1 99 as shown by the accompanying Certificate of Naturalization; that I am the IDENTICAL PERSON described in said Certificate; that I am domiciled in the United States, my permanent residence being at *City of New York* in the State of *New York* where I follow the occupation of *Salesman* that I am about to go abroad temporarily; and that I intend to return to the United States *within two years* with the purpose of residing and performing the duties of citizenship therein.

OATH OF ALLEGIANCE.

Further, I do solemnly swear that I will support and defend the Constitution of the United States against all enemies, foreign and domestic; that I will bear true faith and allegiance to the same; and that I take this obligation freely, without any mental reservation or purpose of evasion : SO HELP ME GOD.

Sworn to before me, this *7th* day of *Sept* 1910 } *Richard Rud. J. Guenther*

John H. Cook

Notary Public.

DESCRIPTION OF APPLICANT.

Age, *38* years.

Stature, *5* feet *3* inches, Eng.

Forehead, *broad*

Eyes, *blue*

Nose, *medium*

Mouth, *medium*

Chin, *round*

Hair, *light*

Complexion, *fair*

Face, *oval*

IDENTIFICATION.

Sept 7 1910

I Hereby Certify, that I know the above named *Richard R. J. Guenther* personally, and know him to be the identical person referred to in the within described Certificate of Naturalization, and that the facts stated in his affidavit are true to the best of my knowledge and belief.

Wm J Mittlesdorf

Address of Witness, *No 1 Broadway*

Applicant desires passport sent to following address:

Richard R J Guenther
80/82 Leonard St
N. Y.

Exhibit 7

Genealogy

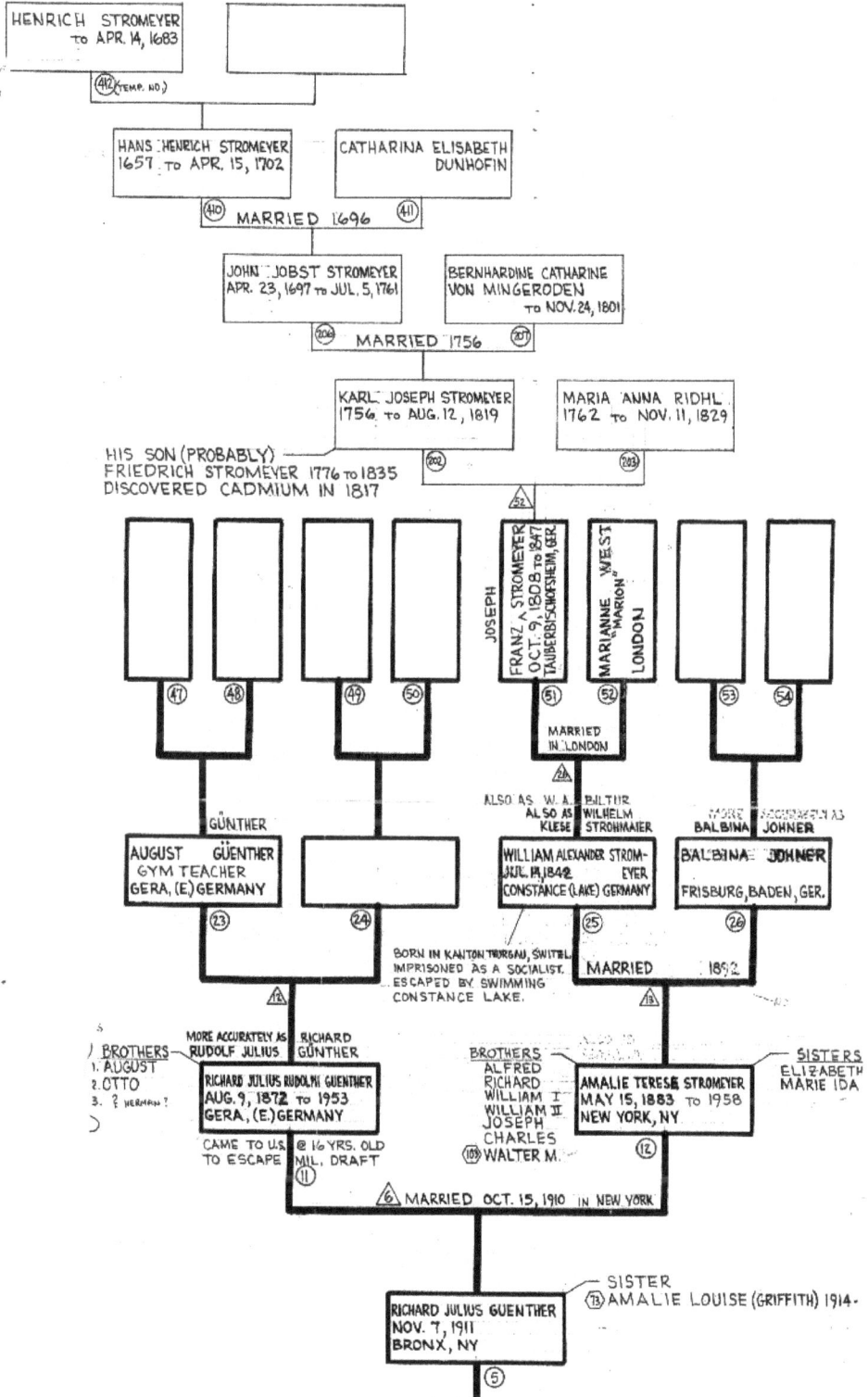

HENRICH STROMEYER
TO APR. 14, 1683
(442) (TEMP. NO.)

HANS HENRICH STROMEYER
1657 TO APR. 15, 1702
(410)

CATHARINA ELISABETH
DUNHOFIN
(411)

MARRIED 1696

JOHN JOBST STROMEYER
APR. 23, 1697 TO JUL. 5, 1761
(208)

BERNHARDINE CATHARINE
VON MINGERODEN
TO NOV. 24, 1801
(207)

MARRIED 1756

KARL JOSEPH STROMEYER
1756 TO AUG. 12, 1819
(202)

MARIA ANNA RIDHL
1762 TO NOV. 11, 1829
(203)

HIS SON (PROBABLY)
FRIEDRICH STROMEYER 1776 TO 1835
DISCOVERED CADMIUM IN 1817

JOSEPH

FRANZ A. STROMEYER
OCT. 9, 1808 TO 1847
TAUBERBISCHOFSHEIM, GER.
(51)

MARIANNE WEST
"MARION"
LONDON
(52)

(47) (48) (49) (50) (53) (54)

MARRIED IN LONDON

ALSO AS W. A. BILTUR
ALSO AS WILHELM
KLESE STROHMAIER

MORE ACCURATELY AS
BALBINA JOHNER

GÜNTHER

AUGUST GÜENTHER
GYM TEACHER
GERA, (E.) GERMANY
(23)

(24)

WILLIAM ALEXANDER STROM-
JUL. 14, 1842 EYER
CONSTANCE (LAKE) GERMANY
(25)

BALBINA JOHNER

FRISBURG, BADEN, GER.
(26)

BORN IN KANTON THURGAU, SWITZL.
IMPRISONED AS A SOCIALIST.
ESCAPED BY SWIMMING
CONSTANCE LAKE.

MARRIED 1892

MORE ACCURATELY AS RICHARD
RUDOLF JULIUS GÜNTHER

BROTHERS
1. AUGUST
2. OTTO
3. ? HERMAN ?

RICHARD JULIUS RUDOLPH GUENTHER
AUG. 9, 1872 TO 1953
GERA, (E.) GERMANY
CAME TO U.S. @ 16 YRS. OLD
TO ESCAPE MIL. DRAFT
(11)

BROTHERS
ALFRED
RICHARD
WILLIAM I
WILLIAM II
JOSEPH
CHARLES
(10) WALTER M.

AMALIE TERESE STROMEYER
MAY 15, 1883 TO 1958
NEW YORK, NY
(12)

SISTERS
ELIZABETH
MARIE IDA

MARRIED OCT. 15, 1910 IN NEW YORK

SISTER
(73) AMALIE LOUISE (GRIFFITH) 1914-

RICHARD JULIUS GUENTHER
NOV. 7, 1911
BRONX, NY
(5)

Exhibit 8

Church of England Marriages and Banns

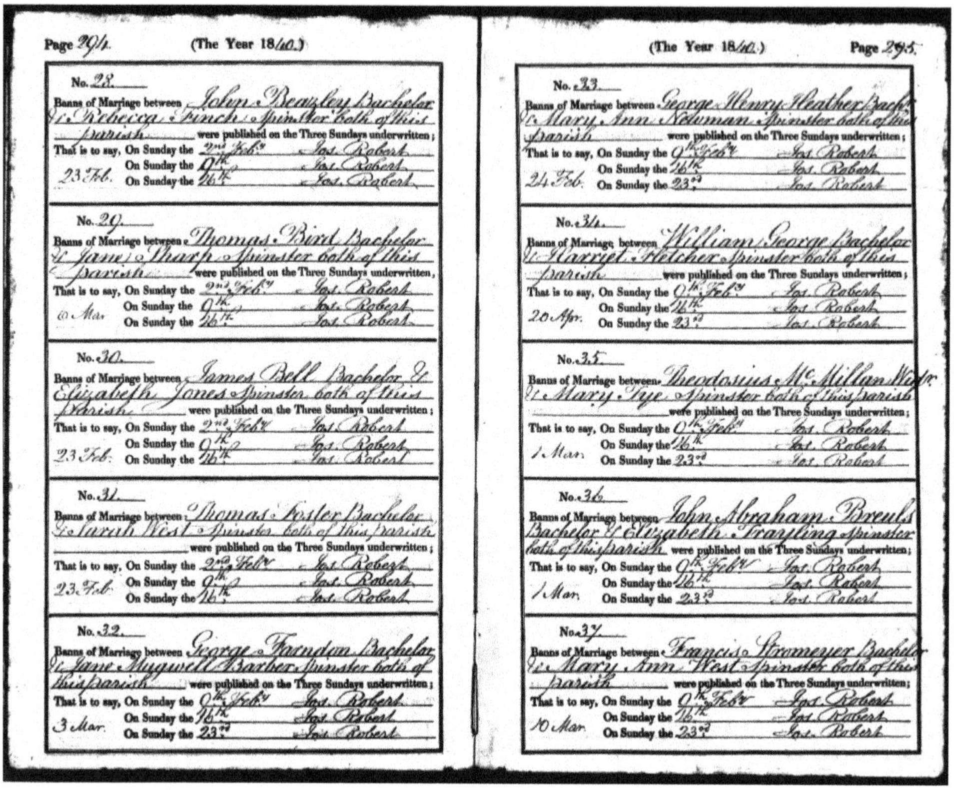

Page 294. (The Year 1840.)

No. 28.
Banns of Marriage between John Beazley Bachelor & Rebecca Finch Spinster both of this parish were published on the Three Sundays underwritten;
That is to say, On Sunday the 2nd Feby Jos. Robert
On Sunday the 9th Jos. Robert
23 Feb. On Sunday the 16th Jos. Robert

No. 29.
Banns of Marriage between Thomas Bird Bachelor & Jane Sharp Spinster both of this parish were published on the Three Sundays underwritten,
That is to say, On Sunday the 2nd Feby Jos. Robert
On Sunday the 9th Jos. Robert
6 Mar On Sunday the 16th Jos. Robert

No. 30.
Banns of Marriage between James Bell Bachelor & Elizabeth Jones Spinster both of this Parish were published on the Three Sundays underwritten;
That is to say, On Sunday the 2nd Feby Jos. Robert
On Sunday the 9th Jos. Robert
23 Feb. On Sunday the 16th Jos. Robert

No. 31.
Banns of Marriage between Thomas Foster Bachelor & Sarah West Spinster both of this parish were published on the Three Sundays underwritten;
That is to say, On Sunday the 2nd Feby Jos. Robert
23 Feb On Sunday the 9th Jos. Robert
On Sunday the 16th Jos. Robert

No. 32.
Banns of Marriage between George Farndon Bachelor & Jane Mugwell Barber Spinster both of this parish were published on the Three Sundays underwritten;
That is to say, On Sunday the 9th Feby Jos. Robert
3 Mar. On Sunday the 16th Jos. Robert
On Sunday the 23rd Jos. Robert

(The Year 1840.) Page 295.

No. 33.
Banns of Marriage between George Henry Heather Bachr & Mary Ann Newman Spinster both of this parish were published on the Three Sundays underwritten;
That is to say, On Sunday the 9th Feby Jos. Robert
On Sunday the 16th Jos. Robert
24 Feb. On Sunday the 23rd Jos. Robert

No. 34.
Banns of Marriage between William George Bachelor & Harriet Fletcher Spinster both of this parish were published on the Three Sundays underwritten;
That is to say, On Sunday the 9th Feby Jos. Robert
On Sunday the 16th Jos. Robert
20 Apr. On Sunday the 23rd Jos. Robert

No. 35.
Banns of Marriage between Theodosius McMillan Widr & Mary Tye Spinster both of this parish were published on the Three Sundays underwritten;
That is to say, On Sunday the 9th Feby Jos. Robert
On Sunday the 16th Jos. Robert
1 Mar. On Sunday the 23rd Jos. Robert

No. 36.
Banns of Marriage between John Abraham Breuls Bachelor & Elizabeth Frayling Spinster both of this parish were published on the Three Sundays underwritten;
That is to say, On Sunday the 9th Feby Jos. Robert
On Sunday the 16th Jos. Robert
1 Mar. On Sunday the 23rd Jos. Robert

No. 37.
Banns of Marriage between Francis Stromeyer Bachelor & Mary Ann West Spinster both of this parish were published on the Three Sundays underwritten;
That is to say, On Sunday the 9th Feby Jos. Robert
On Sunday the 16th Jos. Robert
10 Mar. On Sunday the 23rd Jos. Robert

Exhibit 9

Tales from the wall

THE WELCOME WALL

Here at the end of the world*

Unusual additions to the names on the Welcome Wall are eleven brave Ursuline nuns who helped to pioneer religious education for Catholic girls in rural New South Wales after voyaging from Europe in 1882. Welcome Wall coordinator **Veronica Kooyman** researched their story.

Mother Bernard Wippern (1824–95), first mother superior of the Order of St Ursula in Australia. Born Auguste Wippern in Hildesheim, Hannover. Artist unknown. All images courtesy of OSU

ON A DREARY day in May 1882 a group of nuns, postulants and an aspirant of the Order of St Ursula boarded a sailing ship in Greenwich, England, bound for Armidale in New South Wales to establish a college for rural Catholic girls. The day was auspicious: it was 24 May, the feast day of Our Lady Help of Christians, the patroness of Australia.

The women had already spent five years in exile in England, forced from their cloister in Hannover by the policies of Prussia's 'Iron Chancellor' Otto von Bismarck. How different their lives would be in faraway rural New South Wales where, at the invitation of the Bishop of Armidale, they would establish the Order of St Ursula and begin a vocation for education in Australia. Now, 128 years later, the Ursuline order is celebrating the lives of the women who sailed here by placing the names of 11 of these nuns on the Welcome Wall.

The order originated in a lay organisation founded in 1535 by Angela Merici in northern Italy under the banner of Saint Ursula, a patron of youth and learning. Saint Ursula was a martyr of popular myth, said to have been a fourth-century princess of south-west England betrothed to the pagan governor of Brittany. Sailing to him with an entourage of 11,000 virginal handmaidens, she diverted them on a long European pilgrimage before her wedding. Sadly they reached Cologne as it was being sacked by the Huns, who massacred them all.

The Company of St Ursula developed in a time of unparalleled flowering of literature, art, music and the sciences in Renaissance Italy. Its members were devoted to living a consecrated spiritual life and tending to the needs of others, and teaching catechism to children. By the 17th century the company had spread throughout Italy and to France, where it began educating girls. By 1612 the company had become a teaching order whose members wore a habit, adopted a cloistered life and took solemn vows – one of which was the instruction of girls. It was this vocation that was

to send those women on the long journey to Australia 270 years later.

The order spread further across Europe and in 1700 opened a convent and girls school in Duderstadt, Hannover. During the Napoleonic wars the sisters were forced to leave, but they returned and rebuilt from virtual ruins. Later in the 19th century when Bismarck was unifying Germany, he passed laws that bolstered the power of the secular state at the expense of the Roman Catholic Church. The Ursulines dispersed in 1877, some to England where the order continued the education of girls.

In London some of the nuns met a priest who was to turn the course of these women's lives. Father Elzear Torreggiani from the order of Friars Minor Capuchin, a branch of the Franciscans, was greatly taken by their fate and their devotion to education. Just two years later he was made Bishop of Armidale in New South Wales with a diocese that covered 46,000 square miles.

The colony of New South Wales and its New England region had boomed from the 1850s following discoveries of gold, increased agriculture, industry and migration, but educational opportunities lagged in rural areas. Since the state had suspended funding for religious schools, Bishop Torreggiani turned to religious orders to provide for his largely Irish-Catholic diocese. While the Irish-originated Sisters of Mercy and the Sisters of St Joseph were already established in the diocese, it was the Ursulines whom he invited to begin a college there.

Thirteen women of the order offered to voyage over 10,000 nautical miles to a foreign land they knew almost nothing about, knowing they were unlikely ever to see their homeland again. They were Mother Bernard Wippern, Sr Xavier Graën, Sr Hildegard von Hagen, Sr Ignatius Crone, Sr Cecilia Strohmeyer, Sr Cordula Rowland, Sr Elizabeth Heumann (Kirschenbaur), Sr Agnes Paasch, Sr Thekla Frechmann, Sr Monica Baumann, Sr Joseph Montag, Elise Rhodes and Madame Cecile de Percevale.

The museum's tribute to migrants, The Welcome Wall, encourages
people to recall and record their stories of coming to live in Australia

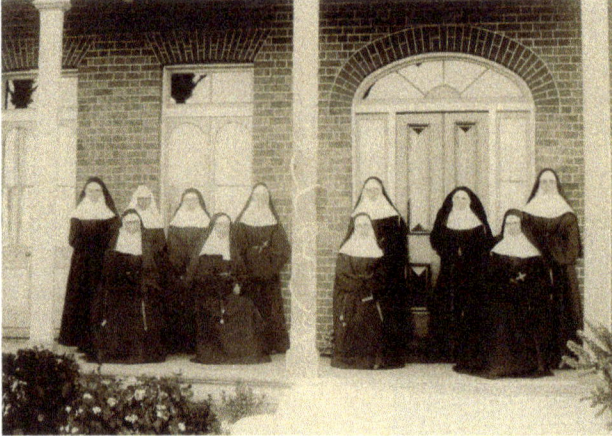

The sisters whose names will be inscribed
on the Welcome Wall. Back row from left:
Sr Thekla, Sr Joseph (as a novice), Sr Elizabeth,
Sr Cordula, Sr Xavier, Sr Monica, Sr Agnes.
Front row from left: Sr Hildegard, Mother Bernard,
Sr Ignatius, and Sr Cecilia.

Tapestry of *Duchess of Edinburgh* made by Sr Mary
(Imelda) Carroll in 2001, after an 1882 painting
by Sr Cordula Rowland. Sr Carroll researched the
ship's flags here at the museum.

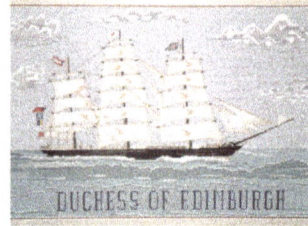

In their writings they referred to their ship *Duchess of Edinburgh* as the 'ark that conveyed the Order to Australia'. The voyage of 14 weeks included three severe storms. Sister Ignatius Crone wrote of 'waves raised mountains high in one part, in another the waters torn asunder like formidable abysses'. Surrounded 'by the grandeurs of the sea and the terrors of the deep... we were hanging, as it were, between two eternities, the Ocean and the Heavens'.

Nevertheless they arrived safely. Sr Ignatius wrote that 'we felt instinctively that our feet were about to tread strange new paths; that a future lay before us more wondrous than we ever dreamed of when we pronounced our vows in the quaint old city of Duderstadt, expecting to live and die within the seclusion of the convent walls'.

In Sydney the women attended the opening ceremony of St Mary's Cathedral, had replaced the original building destroyed by fire in 1865. An overnight steamship passage, a train journey and a very uncomfortable stagecoach ride brought them to the remote town of Armidale, where they began teaching their first classes a week later.

The College of St Ursula, Armidale, became renowned for the rounded education it afforded to young women, with a strong emphasis on cultural activities such as languages, music, art and needlework alongside reading, writing, mathematics and natural sciences. The school quickly became the cultural centre of Armidale, with evening musical and dramatic performances, recitals and art shows. By 1883 the sisters were also responsible for the parish school of nearly 200 boys and girls, while the college was accepting both day students and boarders of all denominations.

There was naturally a cultural divide between the mainly German sisters and the Irish families of the area whom they served. Sister Cordula Rowland, an English woman who had joined the order while it was still in Duderstadt, helped to bridge this divide.

Over the following century the Order of St Ursula branched out to other locations around New South Wales, the ACT and Queensland such as Tweed Heads, Guyra, Dutton Park, Oxley, Ashbury, Toowoomba, Kingsgrove, Macedon, and Canberra. They adapted to the development of state-based education systems and rode the waves of changes to curricula, funding levels and the debates about public, private and religious education. The sisters still work in education but have diversified their activities to include providing services to refugees, migrants and working in parishes.

For the 450th anniversary of the Company of St Ursula, a new breed of rose was propagated in Belgium and named after the founder Angela Merici. It is a beautiful, large, pink rose with a sweet fragrance. Samples were sent to the Australian Ursulines from Rome but were attacked by a fungus while in quarantine. Only one survived – the 'mother rose' from which all the Angela Merici roses in Australia have been cultivated, wherever the Order of St Ursula is to be found. The mother rose still exists in the garden at Ashbury.

The Welcome Wall

It costs just $105 to register a name
and honour your family's arrival in
this great country! We'd love to add
your family's name to The Welcome
Wall, cast in bronze, and place your
story on the online database at
www.anmm.gov.au/ww. So please
don't hesitate to call our staff during
business hours with any enquiries
on 02 9298 3667.

*The title of Sr Mary Kneipp's history of Ursulines in Australia; with thanks to Sr Mary and Sr Colleen Foley for their patient assistance.

Exhibit 10

Catholic Press, *Sydney, Australia, Oct. 10, 1928, p. 29*

Ursuline Convent, Armidale

JUBILEE CELEBRATIONS.

On Saturday, September 28, the golden jubilee of Mother M. Cecilia was celebrated in the Ursuline Convent. Owing to the demands and stress of war-time, there was no public festivity in connection with so unique an event, but numerous friends and ex-pupils sent jubilee gifts, letters and telegrams of felicitation.

His Lordship Dr. O'Connor (Bishop of Armidale) was the celebrant of the 7 o'clock Mass, and the college choir rendered some beautiful singing appropriate to the occasion. At the conclusion of the Mass, and in the presence of his Grace Most Rev. Dr. Redwood (Archbishop of Wellington, N.Z.), the Rev. Mother conducted the jubilarian to the altar steps, where his Lordship read special prayers over her, and crowned her with a gold laurel wreath—symbolic of the accumulated merit of 50 years of devoted, self-sacrificing efforts in the noble cause of instruction of youth. After his Lordship had addressed a brief congratulation to the jubilarian, she was again conducted by the Rev. Mother to her stall, and the Mass of Thanksgiving that followed was said by his Grace Archbishop Redwood.

At midday, the Ursulines entertained at a special dinner the Archbishop of Wellington, N.Z., their Lordships Bishop O'Connor, Bishop Dwyer, Rev. Fathers M. Foley, D. J. Carroll, L. Mahony, Rev. Dr. J. Coleman. Among the congratulatory telegrams received during the day was a much-appreciated one from his Excellency the Apostolic Delegate. It was worded thus:

Mother M. Cecilia, Ursuline Convent, Armidale. Unite with Sisters and pupils, past and present, in celebrating jubilee—fifty golden years of merit and successful labour among God's little ones. Cordially bless you.—APOSTOLIC DELEGATE.

On Monday, 30th ult, three mere candidates were received into the Ursuline Novitiate, alongside of which M. M. Cecilia has laboured in Australia for the past 36 years. Two of the three young ladies received that day are ex-pupils of the Ursulines, viz., Miss Adelaide Fitzgerald, daughter of Mr. Jos. Fitzgerald, of Kunderang Station (now Sister Mary Laurence

O'Toole), and Miss Elizabeth O'Donoghue (Sister Mary Clement Hofbauer), daughter of Mrs. Mary O'Donoghue, Armidale. The third candidate, Miss Gladys Ryan, daughter of Mr. Philip Ryan, Canowindra, received the name of Sister Mary Leonard.

Among the visitors and friends were Mr. and Mrs. Jos. Fitzgerald (Kunderang), Messrs. Desmond, Jas. and Chas. Fitzgerald, the Misses Mary and Flora Fitzgerald, Mrs. W. E. Harris, and Mrs. Williams (Booralong), Mr. and Mrs. Philip Ryan (Canowindra), Mrs. M. O'Donoghue, Mr. John Donoghue, Mr. and Mrs. Jos. Donoghue, Miss M. O'Donoghue, (Armidale), Miss Frecklington, Miss Teefy, Messrs. Geo. and Vincent Frecklington (Canowindra).

His Lordship Dr. O'Connor officiated throughout the impressive ceremony, assisted by the Rev. Father D. J. Carroll. There were also present his Lordship Bishop Dwyer, Rev. Fathers M. Foley, J. Bischoffs, and Rev. Dr. Coleman. At the conclusion of the clothing ceremony, Benediction of the Most Holy Sacrament was given.

On Tuesday night, 1st inst., the boarders of St. Ursula's College presented an exceptionally well-chosen and varied programme to a large audience of friends and visitors. Its purport was to welcome Bishop Dwyer to the diocese and to St. Ursula's, to congratulate M. M. Cecilia on the attainment of her 50th anniversary of holy profession, and also to congratulate the three new Ursulines on their happiness and privileges. Space precludes detailing the items on the programme; each item had its merits, its special import and message. The long programme was all too short for such an appreciative audience. At the conclusion congratulatory speeches were made by Bishop O'Connor, Bishop Dwyer, and Dr. W. E. Harris.

So great was the enthusiastic appreciation of the audience that by special request of Bishop O'Connor the programme was again presented to his Grace Archbishop Duhig and his Lordship Bishop Shiel on Wednesday afternoon, 2nd inst., who arrived in Armidale at midnight on Tuesday. Their eulogies, added to those of the day previous, were more than reward to teachers and pupils in their efforts to entertain. It was one of the most artistically-finished entertainments of the year.

The pupils of St. Ursula's College presented to the venerated jubilarian a magnificent brass crucifix for High Altar use, suitably inscribed, as a jubilee memento.

Exhibit 11

Armidale Chronicle, Sat., July 14, 1928

The Ursulines.

DEATH OF MOTHER MARY CECELIA STROMEYER.

THE LAST OF THE PIONEERS.

At the Ursuline Convent, Armidale, on Wednesday morning, July 11, occurred the death of Mother Mary Cecelia Stromeyer, the last of the Pioneer Ursulines of the Armidale Foundation. She was within two months of the celebration of her Diamond Jubilee of Holy Profession.

The deceased Religious was born at Citeaux. In 1842, at the age of 18 years, she became a convert to the Catholic faith. She was received into the Ursuline Novitiate at Duderstadt, Germany, and was professed on September 28, 1868.

Driven from Germany by the Kulturkampf of Bismarck, she sought refuge in France, whence she crossed to England to rejoin her Sister-exiles at Greenwich. After five years spent in England, she was one of the small band of brave hearts who volunteered to cross the ocean in order to labour for God's glory in distant Australia. Under the paternal care of the Right Rev. Elzear Torreggianl, O.S.F.C., Bishop of Armidale, the Ursulines once more took up the labours of their institute in a foreign land. They had influential friends in England who had taken the keenest interest in their welfare, but these they had bravely sacrificed in their zeal for the souls of children in a far-off mission field. Such sacrifices do not pass unrewarded. From the moment of their landing in Australia, a kindly welcome awaited them personally at the hands of the saintly Mother-General, Mother Mary of the Cross, at Mount-street Convent, North Sydney (the Mother House of the Sisters of St. Joseph).

From Sydney the exiles travelled by rail to Uralla, and then took coach for Armidale, as the northern railway line had not then been completed beyond the former town.

The heartiest of greetings was accorded the travellers by the good people of Armidale, who always showed them the greatest kindness. Numbers of pupils came for lessons in music, art, and the like subjects, and soon the Nuns found themselves busy and happy among their loved charges.

During the long years that elapsed after their arrival in 1882, none was more active in the work of Christian education than the late Mother M. Cecelia. For many years she was Mistress of Studies in St. Ursula's College, and at one period she was Mistress of Boarders. In every case she won the love and admiration of her pupils, whose loyalty to the deceased Mother was proved by their letters written to her even up to the time of her death by some who had been her earliest pupils in Armidale.

In 1918, Mother M. Cecelia celebrated her golden jubilee of profession. During her last illness the late Mother M. Cecelia was frequently visited by his Lordship, Right Rev. Dr. O'Connor, and the local clergy. She retained consciousness almost till her last moment, and had the happiness of receiving the Last Absolutions from the devoted Priest who arrived just as she breathed her last sigh.

The Ursuline Community desire to return sincere thanks to his Lordship and the Armidale priests, to Dr. Brydon, Nurse Gillett, and their many kind friends and sympathisers.

The funeral left the Convent Chapel at 11 o'clock on Thursday, July 12.

DEATH OF MOTHER MARY CECELIA STROMEYER
THE LAST OF THE PIONEERS.

At the Ursuline Convent, Armidale, on Wednesday morning, July 11, occurred the death of Mother Mary Cecelia Stromeyer, the last of the Pioneer Ursulines of the Armidale Foundation. She was within two months of the celebration of her Diamond Jubilee of Holy Profession.

The deceased Religious was born at Citeaux. In 1842, at the age of 18 years, she became a convert to the Catholic faith. She was received into the Ursuline Novitiate at Duderstadt, Germany, and was professed on September 28, 1868.

Driven from Germany by the Kulturkampf of Bismarck, she sought refuge in France, whence she crossed to England to rejoin her Sister-exiles at Greenwich. After live years spent in England, she was one of the small hand of brave hearts who volunteered to cross the ocean in order to labour for God's glory In distant Australia, tender the paternal care of the Right Rev. Elzear Torreggianl, O.S.F.C., Bishop of Armidale, the Ursulines once more took up the labours of their institute in a foreign land. They had Influential friends in England who had taken the keenest interest in their welfare, but these they had bravely sacrificed in their zeal for the souls of children in a far-off mission field. Such sacrifices do not pass unrewarded. From the moment of their landing in Australia, a kindly welcome, awaited them personally at the hands of the saintly Mother General Mother Mary of the Cross, at Mount-street Convent, North Sydney (the Mother House of the Sisters of St. Joseph).

From Sydney the exiles travelled by rail to Uralla, and then took coach for Armidale, as the northern railway line had not then been completed beyond the former town.

The heartiest of greetings was accorded the travelers by the good people of Armidale, who always showed them the greatest kindness. Numbers of pupils came for lessons in music, art, and the like subjects, and soon the Nuns found themselves busy and happy among their loved charges.

During the long years that elapsed after their arrival in 1882, none was more active in the work of Christian education than the late Mother M. Cecelia. For many years she was Mistress of Studies in St. Ursula's College, and at one period she was Mistress of Boarders. In every case she won the love and admiration of her pupils, whose loyalty to the deceased Mother was proved by their letters written to her even up to the lime of her death by some who had been her earliest pupils in Armidale.

In 1918, Mother M. Cecelia celebrated her golden jubilee of profession. During her last illness the late Mother M. Cecelia was frequently visited by his Lordship, Bight Rev. Dr. O'Connor, and the local clergy. She retained consciousness almost till her last moment, and had the happiness of receiving the Last Absolutions from the devoted Priest who arrived Just as she breathed her last sigh.

The Ursuline Community desire to return sincere thanks to his Lordship and the Armidale priests, to Dr. Brydon, Nurse Gillett, and their many kind friends and sympathizers.

The funeral left the Convent Chapel at II o'clock on Thursday, July 12.

Exhibit 12

Griffith Family Bible

Family Record. of Isaac and Eliza Griffith

BIRTHS.	BIRTHS.
William C Griffith son of Isaac & Eliza Griffith was born the 19th day of January 1840	Winfield Scott Griffith son of Isaac and Eliza Griffith was born on the 18th day of June 1848
John Griffith Son of Isaac & Eliza Griffith was born on the 24th day of March 1841	Isaac Newton son of Isaac and Eliza Griffith was born on the fifth day of February 1852
John James Griffith and Margaret Ann Griffith was born on the 2d day of May 1843 Son and dorter of Isaac & Eliza Griffith	Spencer Vinton Griffith son of Isaac and Eliza Griffith was born on the 9th day of may in the year 1853
Thomas Alfred Griffith son of Isaac and Eliza Griffith was born on the 26th day of December 1844	Augustus Franklin Griffith son of Isaac and Eliza Griffith was born on the 23d day of April 1858
George Milton Griffith son of Isaac and Eliza Griffith was born on the fifth day of may 1846	

DEATHS.

John Griffith son of Isaac and Eliza Griffin departed this life on the 15th day of December 1841

Thomas Alfred Griffitt son of Isaac And Eliza Griffitt departed this life on the 25th day of august 1853

Isaac Newton Griffith son of Isaac and Eliza Griffith. departed this life on the 22nd day of April 1854.

Augustus Franklin Griffith son of Isaac and Eliza Griffith departed this life on the 22d day of August 1860.

George Milton Griffith son of Isaac and Eliza Griffith departed this life on the fifth day of August 1864

DEATHS.

Isaac Griffith son of James and Margarett Griffith departed this life on the 21st day of October 1866

Spencer Vinton Griffith son of Isaac and Eliza Griffith departed this life on the 3d day of January 1868.

Margarett Ann Griffith daughter of Isaac and Eliza Griffith departed this life on the 16th of July 1868.

Eliza Griffith departed this life on the 7th day of February, 1886. She was the beloved wife of Isaac Griffith, and in the 73d year of her age.

John James Griffith son of Isaac and Eliza Griffith departed this life on the 7th of February 1893

MARRIAGES.

Isaac and Eliza Griffith was Married on the 9th day of April 1839 By the [?]

DEATHS

Eliza Griffith, wife of Isaac Griffith, departed this life Feb 7th 1886

Winfield Scott Griffith son of Isaac and Eliza Griffith departed this life on the 17th day of April 1900.

William Curtis Griffith son of Isaac and Eliza Griffith departed this life on the 27th day of April 1913. At 3.10 d. M.

Frederika Royston Griffith died date unknown

MARRIAGES.

William C. Griffith and Frederika Royston married 1875 (?) see letter 4/20/37

Albert Spencer Griffith son of William and Frederika Griffith.

Howard Ernest Griffith son of William and Frederika Griffith born January 3, 1877.

William C. Griffith married Julia B. Harbaugh.

Ruth Esther Griffith daughter of William C. and Julia B. Griffith Died 3/25/26

Howard E. Griffith married Florence Phillips 1913?

Charles E Griffith born 2/28/15

Charles Ernest Griffith married Amalie Louise Guenther 9/16/36 died 2/27/00

Charles E Griffith Jr. son of Charles and Amalie Griffith born 9/12/37

Alan Richard Griffith son of Charles and Amalie Griffith born 12/17/41

Family Record.

BIRTHS.	BIRTHS.
David Edward Griffith son of Charles & Amelia Griffith born 10/28/53	Marriages

Charles Ernest Griffith Jr. married Susan Wilkins 1962

Alan Richard Griffith married Elizabeth Ferguson 1964

David Edward Griffith married Jacqueline McEwen married 1979

Charles E. Griffith Senior married Mary Frances Galvin December 29, 2000 |

Exhibit 13

GRIFFITH.—At his residence, No. 142 East Monument street, on the 21st of October, of paralysis, ISAAC GRIFFITH, aged 58 years and 2 months.—[Cincinnati papers please copy.]

Baltimore Sun, *Oct. 22, 1866, p. 2.*

GRIFFITH.—On the morning of January 3d, 1868, at the residence of his parents, No. 142 East Monument street, Baltimore, SPENCER VINTON GRIFFITH, aged 14 years 7 months and 24 days, son of Isaac and Eliza Griffith.

Baltimore Sun, *Jan. 4, 1868, p. 2.*

GRIFFITH.—July 16th, 1868, at No. 142 East Monument street, MAGGIE A. GRIFFITH, only daughter of Isaac and Eliza Griffith, aged 25 years 2 months and 15 days.

Baltimore Sun, *July 17, 1868, p. 2.*

GRIFFITH.—The funeral services of Mrs. ELIZA GRIFFITH, whose death was announced in yesterday's Sun, will be held in the M. E. Church, Mount Carmel, Baltimore county, at one o'clock tomorrow Wednesday afternoon. Relatives and friends are invited to attend.

Baltimore Sun, *Feb. 9, 1886, p. 2.*

Mr. John J. Griffith, fifty years old, was found dead in his bedroom with a pistol bullet in his brain last Tuesday morning, at the house of Mrs. George L. Lloyd, on the York road, a mile north of Hereford, where he boarded. Justice John F. Heisse held an inquest, and the jury gave a verdict of suicide. The body was found lying between the bed and nightstand, and it is believed that Mr. Griffith stood before the glass and fired the pistol. The ball entered the right temple. Letters were found on the table which showed that suicide had been contemplated since last September, the reasons given being bad health, poverty and destitution. One letter directed that he be buried at Mount Carmel, fifth district. Mr. Griffith was a book agent, and he had been a teacher at Texas, Baltimore county, and at Scheib's school, in the city. He has many relatives in Baltimore county. One brother, Rev. W. C. Griffith, lives in Hagerstown.

Baltimore Sun, *Feb. 9, 1893, p. 7.*

Exhibit 14

Baltimore Sun, *Sept. 25, 1900, p. 9*

THE TRUST EVILS

Views Of A Minister On The Serious Question Of The Hour.

[Special Dispatch to the Baltimore Sun.]
HAGERSTOWN, MD., Sept. 24.—Rev. W. O. Griffith, of Hagerstown, lawyer, poet, author, lecturer and a minister of the Methodist Episcopal Church, a Republican in politics and a gentleman of wide observation, in an interview with THE SUN correspondent, says that in his opinion the trust question is the most serious in this campaign, and he believes many voters will hold the Republican party responsible for their growth and the evils they entail. He stated that the wealth of the country is gradually getting into the hands of the few, and that nearly all the millionaires and trust magnates are now supporting the Republican party, which seems to be fathering them. Rev. Mr. Griffith said:

"What do I think of the present aspect of the campaign? Well, the battle seems now to be raging in the West. There the spellbinders have congregated in great force. Beyond an occasional skirmish in Maryland and West Virginia, the South is too much one-sided to encourage invasion. The divisions of 1896 have apparently disappeared and

"Those opposed eyes that, like the meteors of a
   troubled heaven, did lately meet in the intestine shock,
Shall now, in mutual, well-beseeming ranks, march
   all one way.

"Will imperialism have more influence than the free-silver question? No one can tell. Between the two, the former seems to claim the most attention in papers and magazines. Even the President devoted a great deal of time to it in his letter of acceptance. A recent writer declares that imperialism is in the air and that it is spreading over the country, without regard to party views; that the people have been acquiescing in Executive acts, and tacitly recognizing the use of Executive power, for which no warrant can be found in the Constitution. It would seem to be only natural that in the progress of the country the Presidential office should assume more importance than formerly. The Cabinet is much larger, the duties of the President more extended, and as the country grows and expands the President is more looked to as the central power of government.

"Congress has not grown relatively in the eyes of the world, and in times of trouble the question usually asked is, What will the President do? If his action corresponds with what the people think right, but few stop to inquire whether he acted within the authority of the Constitution.

"When Andrew Jackson removed the public funds from the United States Bank very many believed the act without authority, but the people approved, and there the matter ended.

"When President Lincoln suspended the habeas corpus act during the Civil War Chief Justice Taney declared his action unconstitutional, but the military necessity for such a course was believed to justify the President and opposition ceased.

"Today the papers are discussing the authority of the President to act as he has in China and the Philippines, and it is certainly a very important question, which should be pondered over by all who are capable of considering it; but, notwithstanding its importance, by far the greater number of voters will be governed by the other questions, namely: Did he do right? Was it for the general good? Will it prove beneficial?

"What do I think of the trust problem? It is the most serious question before the country today. I once heard the late Senator Ingalls say that he did not believe any man ever earned a million dollars honestly. But however the enormous aggregations of capital may have arisen, there can be no doubt of their power for evil. They stand opposed to that equality of opportunity which is one of the great blessings in a democratic government. Goldsmith has aptly portrayed the change of conditions now occurring in his 'Deserted Village.'

"Ill fares the land to hastening ills a prey,
Where wealth accumulates and men decay;

   *   *   *   *   *

A time there was ere England's griefs began,
When every rood of ground maintained its man,
For him light Labor spread her wholesome store,
Just gave what life required, but gave no more;
His best companions, innocence and health,
And his best riches, ignorance of wealth.
But times are altered. Trade's unfeeling trains
Usurp the land and dispossess the swain."

Exhibit 15

Baltimore Sun, *April 28, 1913, p. 2*

REV. W. C. GRIFFITH DEAD

Retired Methodist Minister, He Also Practiced Law And Lectured.

Hagerstown, Md., April 27.—Rev. W. C. Griffith, 79 years old, the oldest minister in the Baltimore Conference, Methodist Episcopal Church, died today of paralysis at his home in Hagerstown. For about two years he had been practically helpless. Mr. Griffith served a number of pastorates in Maryland and Virginia and for a time practiced law in Hagerstown and Baltimore county. He founded the Blue Ridge Outlook, a weekly publication, about 15 years ago, but the paper had a brief existence. During his practice of law he conducted a number of cases against saloon keepers. He was author of several works of fiction and philosophy. He also lectured on the experiences of a West Virginia circuit rider.

Mr. Griffith was born in Baltimore county and for many years was teacher of languages in the old Scheib's School in Baltimore. His first wife before marriage was Miss Frederica Royston, of Baltimore county. Her surviving children are H. Ernest Griffith, of Baltimore, and Prof. A. S. Griffith, of Palmyra, N. J. His second wife, who was Miss Hargrove, of Pen-Mar, and one daughter, Miss Ruth Griffith, survive.

Exhibit 16

Baltimore Sun, *June 5, 1912, p. 7*

Here To Escape Eastern Shoremen

SHERIFF TULL AND HIS PRISONER, WESLEY MILES, COLORED

Baltimore Sun, *Dec. 6, 1912, p. 2*

SHERIFF ELUDES MOBS

Lands Negro From Princess Anne In City Jail.

PURSUED IN THREE COUNTIES

Night Race In Automobiles, Detours Around Towns And Hiding Place In Woods Figure In Flight.

Wesley Miles, the negro charged with criminal assault upon Maggie Phillips, the 14-year-old daughter of former Sheriff William J. Phillips, of Princess Anne, Somerset county, was brought to the Baltimore City Jail shortly after noon yesterday by Sheriff Harding P. Tull, of that county.

The negro had been chased all Monday night by infuriated man-hunters from three counties. He would have been lynched the moment this mob had him in its power. His life was saved by the promptness and ingenuity of Sheriff Tull, Deputy Sheriff E. O. Townsend, State's Attorney Gordon Tull and Washington Revell, of that county.

Miles, in a stammering and shifty manner, denied his guilt when questioned at the jail. He said he had been working for Mr. Phillips about two years and had worked for him about 20 years ago. He declared that if guilty he would have left the scene of the crime promptly.

Both Sheriff Tull and his prisoner were nearly exhausted when they reached the jail. The story of how the officers used automobiles and hid in a woods in Delaware to elude the determined pursuers who had gathered from Somerset and Wicomico counties, Maryland and Sussex county, Delaware, is one of stirring incidents.

Part Played By Autos.

The Sheriff, with his party, left Princess Anne in an automobile Monday night for Salisbury, the prisoner crouching in the tonneau of the machine. At Fruitland, near Salisbury, they stopped for gasoline and learned that pursuing parties had set out from Princess Anne after them. As their machine was slow, they abandoned it and secured a larger and faster car.

Taking a swing around Salisbury, the Sheriff headed straight for Delaware, hoping to reach Seaford in time to catch a northbound train over the New York, Philadelphia and Norfolk Railroad. He learned, however, that a crowd was waiting for him at Seaford and doubled back to head for Delmar or Cambridge. Mobs were at both places, he learned.

Turning north again, the resourceful Sheriff made another detour around a town—Seaford this time—and hurried on toward Greenwood. He had changed his route to Baltimore. Figuring that the pursuers would expect him to board a New York, Philadelphia and Norfolk train for Wilmington and would be on guard at various stations, he decided to take a Maryland, Delaware and Virginia train at Greenwood and come to Baltimore by way of Love Point.

He dared not venture into Greenwood in the automobile, however, and several hours before daylight dismissed the machine, hiding in the woods with the deputy sheriff and the negro. While there they heard several parties, thought to be pursuers, pass.

Got Team From Farmer.

The party crept cautiously from the woods at daybreak. There was a little farmhouse near and Tull awoke the farmer, whose name he did not know. There they secured a team.

With this they got to Greenwood in time to catch the train to Love Point. No one molested them at the station and no one on the train had heard of the crime or the pursuit. The officers were constantly on guard against interference in Caroline and Queen Anne's counties. They could have been headed off by telegraph, but none of the pursuers thought of their taking this route to safety and they were undisturbed.

At Love Point the steamer Westmoreland took aboard the fugitives and for the first time the party felt safe.

Sheriff Needed Rest.

Landing at Pier 7, Light Street Wharf, about noon, the Sheriff and his prisoner, both completely tired out, walked to Charles street and boarded a car, changing at Fayette street for the city jail. Soon after the big gates had been opened by Keeper Revell Warden Lee received the negro and relieved Sheriff Tull of his dangerous charge. The Sheriff did not tarry long, but explained that he had to return to Somerset county to get an order of court for the Baltimore authorities to hold Miles until the trial. He said he would get some rest before starting back to Princess Anne.

Exciting, Says Officer.

After delivering Miles to Warden Lee, at the city jail, Sheriff Tull went to the home of his uncle, Mr. Alonzo L. Miles, 205 West Lanvale street, where he told of his flight with the negro.

"I was a deputy sheriff six years before being elected to my present office," he said, "and I have had many exciting experiences, but the flight of last night eclipsed them all. I knew well that if the men from Somerset once got their hands on Miles he was a doomed man.

"I knew, too, that they would get all the speed they could from their machines, but we had a good two hours' start and that counted for something. We made straight for Delmar after leaving Salisbury, and then passed on toward Seaford, where I hoped to get a train for Wilmington. Before arriving at Seaford, however, I learned that a mob had gathered there and I changed my route. Revell knew the roads well and I told him to try and make a station on the Love Point line.

"Greenwood was the first station of any size, and we arrived there about 3 o'clock in the morning. I told Revell to take the machine back and we camped in the woods not far from the station until the first morning train came along.

"We then got a team at Greenwood, hurried up to the station and got aboard the train a minute before it left. I got my man on board the Westmoreland at Love Point and felt greatly relieved when I landed in Baltimore."

Sheriff Tull, Deputy Sheriff Townsend and State's Attorney Tull, of Somerset, left the city yesterday afternoon on the Peninsula Express for Princess Anne.

Baltimore Sun, *Oct. 12, 1912, p. 14*

SOMERSET NEGRO GUILTY

Wesley Miles Convicted Of Assaulting Ex-Sheriff's Daughter.

TO PENITENTIARY OR DEATH

Judge Gorter Suspends Sentence Until Today—Accused Is Not Put On Witness Stand.

Wesley Miles, the negro charged with felonious assault in Somerset county on a 14-year-old white girl and brought to the Baltimore jail to prevent lynching, was convicted of the crime yesterday in Criminal Court No. 2.

The penalty is from 18 months to 21 years in the penitentiary or death. Judge Gorter suspended sentence until today. After deliberating 25 minutes the jury rendered the verdict at 6.15 P. M., finding Miles guilty on the first count of the indictment.

Maggie Phillips, the daughter of former Sheriff William J. Phillips, of Princess Anne, was the victim of Miles. The negro was employed to work about the store of Mr. Phillips. May 28 last the girl was sent by her mother to the third story of their home, near the store, to pack some winter clothing. It is alleged that the negro followed her and kept her a prisoner in the attic for about half an hour.

Threatened To Kill Her.

By threatening to kill her and her mother if she told what he had done and brandishing a knife at the same time, it was alleged, the negro terrorized the girl so that she did not say anything about the assault until she told her mother the following Sunday night.

When the girl's story became public the negro was brought to Baltimore by roundabout ways to escape lynching parties after him. His case was subsequently removed here for trial, and C. O. Melvin, a lawyer, of Pocomoke, was assigned by the Somerset County Court as counsel for the defense. State's Attorney Gordon Tull, of Somerset county, and Assistant State's Attorney Harry W. Nice prosecuted the case.

Girl In Court.

Although 14 years old, the jury was told that the girl has only the intelligence of one several years younger. She looked pretty in court, dressed in white, with a big blue hat.

Miles was not put on the witness stand, and no one was called to testify for him. He is about 50 years old, short and chunky, and has a wife and eight children. He was dressed in an old patched suit of clothes, with no collar to his colored shirt. His nervousness was frequently manifested. Attorney Melvin argued to the jury that the silence of the girl for a week after the assault and the fact that Miles did not run away, but remained on the scene, were facts that should convince them that the negro was not guilty of the crime charged.

Jury In The Case.

The jury which tried the case was as follows:

Charles Bull, 306 East Lafayette avenue.
Frank McLean, 115 North Fulton avenue.
Ernest Johannsen, 2050 Orleans street.
William Neuhaus, 2012 Canton avenue.
Leonard J. Nilson, 1332 Hanover street.
C. Harry Reeves, 926 N. Charles street.
Nelson Tinsley, 2841 Pennsylvania ave.
William R. Hall, 2727 West North avenue.
George W. Kerner, 1517 West Fayette street.
Ernest Meinfelder, 2010 Orleans street.
Edgar L. Green, 2058 Kennedy avenue.
Howard J. King, 27 North Luzerne street.

Exhibit 17

Marylander and Herald *(Princess Anne, Md.), Mar. 15, 1921, p. 1*

William J. Phillips Dead

Mr. William J. Phillips died at his home in Princess Anne last Friday night, about 9 o'clock, of Bright's disease, in the 63rd year of his age.

Mr. Phillips had been an invalid for about 8 months and had been confined to his home for four weeks. He was well known throughout Somerset county and during his life owned considerable property in this town upon which he erected many houses. He also had a number of dwellings built on his lots on "Somerset Heights" before he disposed of the property some two years ago. He was elected sheriff of Somerset county on the Democratic ticket in November, 1909, which office he held until November, 1911. The deceased was a member of the Junior Order United American Mechanics, Improved Order Red Men and the Daughters of America.

Mr. Phillips is survived by his widow, who, before her marriage, was Miss Florence Pollitt, and three sons (Messrs. Clarence W. Phillips, of Princess Anne; William Roger and J. Weldon Phillips, of Chester, Pa.) and three daughters (Misses Ada A., Margaret E. and Annie H. Phillips, all of Chester, Pa.).

Funeral services were held last Sunday afternoon in Manokin Presbyterian Church, conducted by the Rev. Walter Arcubult, rewr of Somerset parish. Interment was in the course cemetery. The pallbearers were, Messrs. Gordon Tull, Wm. P. Todd, Howard Anderson, S. Upshur Long, George W. Brown and Harry C. Dashiell.

Exhibit 18

Delaware County Daily Times *(Chester, Penn.), Aug. 14, 1951, p. 2*

Mrs. Florence A. Phillips

Born in Maryland

Mrs. Florence A. Phillips, widow of William J. Phillips, died this morning at the residence of her daughter, Mrs. J. H. Jett, 12 W. 8th st., after a two-month illness.

Born in Somerset County, Md., she was the daughter of the late Josiah and Amanda Pollitt. She had lived in Chester for the last 30 years.

Mrs. Phillips' leaves three sons, Clarence W. Phillips, Princess Anne, Md.; William R. Phillips, 921 E. 16th st., and J. Weldon Phillips, 638 9th av., Prospect Park; two daughters, Mrs. Ada P. Jett, with whom she made her home at 12 W. 8th st., and Mrs. Anne P. Van Zandt, 2306 Upland st.

Also surviving are seven grandchildren, C. Wilson Phillips Jr., Preston, Md.; George Lee Phillips, Anniston, Ala.; Robert W. and James ꓤ. VanZant and Jerry P. Brown, Chester; James W. Phillips Jr., and Marlyn E. Phillips, Prospect Park, and four great-grandchildren.

Friends may call Wednesday evening from 7 to 9 at the Ray F. Imschweller funeral home, 1600 Edgmont av. Services will be at the convenience of the family at Princess Anne, Md.

Exhibit 19

Marylander and Herald (Princess Anne, Md.), Feb. 17, 1920, p. 1

Death Of Miss Nellie Phillips

Miss Nellie Frances Phillips, daughter of Mr. and Mrs. William J. Phillips, formerly of Princess Anne, but now of Chester, Pa., died at the home of Mrs. S. E. Wheeler, in Baltimore, Sunday evening, February 8th.

Miss Phillips was 24 years old and had not been in the best of health for the past three years. On Wednesday, February 4th, her condition became serious and on Saturday pneumonia developed and she sank rapidly until the end came. Miss Phillips was born in Princess Anne and attended Washington High School and Beacom Business College, Salisbury. She finished her education in Baltimore where, she has resided for the past seven years. At the time of her death she was private secretary of the Fidelity Finance Corporation in that city.

Besides her parents she is survived by three sisters (Misses Ada Adella, Margaret Elizabeth and Anna Hitch Phillips, of Chester, Pa.), and three brothers (Messrs. Wm. Roger Phillips, James Weldon Phillips, of Chester, Pa., and Clarence Wilson Phillips, of Princess Anne).

Her remains were brought to Princess Anne last Tuesday and taken to the residence of her uncle and aunt, Mr. and Mrs. S. C. Long. Funeral services were held in St. Andrew's Church last Wednesday morning at 10 30 o'clock, conducted by the Rev. O. H. Murphy. The interment was in Manokin Presbyterian Church cemetery. The pallbearers were: Messrs. Mark L. Costen, Harold A. McAllen, Roy P. Stagg, Jessie M. Pollett and Clarence Wilson and Wm. Roger Phillips, her two brothers.

Appendix
The Next Generation

1. **CHARLES E. GRIFFITH JR.** married, first, **SUSAN JANE WILKINS** (May 11, 1939–March 25, 1973), daughter of ROGER CARSON WILKINS and EVELYN ELIZABETH McFADDEN, in June 1962, and had three children. He later married **NANCY JANE KENNINGTON** (August 27, 1948–), the daughter of CHARLES HENRY KENNINGTON JR. and DORIS BRADSHAW HUSTON, on June 25, 1983 in Princeton, New Jersey.

    Children of Charles E. Griffith Jr. and Susan Jane (Wilkins):

    — JENNIFER ANN GRIFFITH, born January 24, 1963, married BRIAN DEAN BLACK (born May 12, 1960), son of HARRY LYNN BLACK and WINNIE CAROLYN GENTRY, on May 22, 1993 in Rumson, New Jersey. They have the following children:

    - CARSON WILKINS BLACK, born July 3, 1995.

    - SUSAN GENTRY BLACK, born July 26, 1997.

    — CHARLES ERNEST GRIFFITH III, born June 4, 1964, married JEANNE MARIE BILBAO, daughter of JEANNIE MARIE VINCENT and PHILIP FRANCIS BILBAO, on August 24, 1991 in Chappaqua, New York. They have the following children:

    - KATHRYN WILKINS GRIFFITH, born September 24, 1992.

    - THOMAS CHARLES McFADDEN GRIFFITH, born October 12, 1995.

    - JOHN ROGER GRIFFITH, born September 19, 1998.

    — KATHLEEN McKENZIE GRIFFITH, born July 18, 1969, married STEPHEN POTTER (born July 10, 1968), son of ELLEN HARTLEY and HOWARD POTTER, on August 20, 1994 in Peru, New

York (divorced January 16, 2014). They have the following children:

- McKenzie Kennington Griffith Potter, born January 14, 1996.

- Bray Guenther Griffith Potter, born July 31, 1999.

2. **Alan Richard Griffith** married **Elizabeth Spencer Ferguson** (born January 17, 1943), daughter of Spencer Ferguson and Elizabeth Phillips Lea, on November 28, 1964 in Cincinnati, Ohio.

Children of Alan Richard Griffith and Elizabeth Spencer Ferguson:

— Timothy Spencer Griffith, born May 11, 1967, married Anne Elizabeth Corso (born March 2, 1971), daughter of Gayle Parsons McLaughlin, on June 16, 2012 in Centreville, Maryland.

— Elizabeth Amalie Griffith, born June 29, 1971, married Thomas Herbert Hipp (born August 5, 1971), son of Herbert Richard Hipp and Elizabeth Betts, on April 27, 1996 in Lawrenceville, New Jersey. They have the following children:

- Amalie Elizabeth Hipp, born September 28, 1999.

- Henry Thomas Hipp, born September 28, 1999.

3. **David Edward Griffith** married **Jacqueline McEwen** (born April 22, 1955), daughter of Joseph McEwen and Margaret A. Grady, on April 21, 1979 in Huntingdon Valley, Pennsylvania.

Children of David Edward Griffith and Jacqueline McEwen:

— Lindsay Anne Griffith, born November 16, 1987, married Daniel Jonathan Shapiro (born December 14, 1984), son of David Shapiro and Lindsay Stam, on June 18, 2016 in New York, New York.

— Ian Thomsen Griffith, born April 21, 1991, married Skylyre Lea Wenhold (born April 20, 1993), daughter of Heather Ventura and Eric Wenhold, on October 7, 2019 in Blue Bell, Pennsylvania. They have the following child:

- Sage C. Carl Wenhold, born June 10, 2015.

Index

Numbers in *italics* refer to pages with images.
Numbers in **bold** refer to family tree charts.

www.ingramcontent.com/pod-product-compliance
Lightning Source LLC
Chambersburg PA
CBHW041609260326
41914CB00012B/1435